VICTORIAN

CROSS STITCH
SAMPLERS

VICTORIAN

CROSS STITCH SAMPLERS

Angela Wainwright

CASSELL

A CASSELL BOOK

First published 1995
by Cassell
Wellington House
125 Strand
London WC2R 0BB

Produced by Rosemary Wilkinson
4 Lonsdale Square
London N1 1EN

Distributed in the United States
by Sterling Publishing Co., Inc.
387 Park Avenue South, New York,
New York 10016-8810

Distributed in Australia
By Capricorn Link (Australia) Pty Ltd
2/13 Carrington Road
Castle Hill
NSW 2154

Design and chart artwork: Pentrix Design
Photography: Mark Gatehouse
Illustrations: Stephen Dew
Picture research: Jane Lewis
Sampler mounts: Delia Elliman
Colour reproduction: Tenon & Polert Ltd

British Library Cataloguing-in-Publication Data
A catalogue record for this book is available from the British Library

ISBN 0-304-34440-0 (hardback)
ISBN 0-304-34693-4 (paperback)

Printed and bound in Italy

Contents

Historical Background

The Victorian period was one of unprecedented contrasts practically and idealistically: there were extremes of wealth and poverty; a quest both for a revival of past design styles and a new style for the era; and while homage was paid to accelerated industrial development on the one hand, there was a complete rejection of it on the other. Some people decry it as an age of eclectic muddle, others praise it as a wonderful fusion of the new and the old.

Exploring the four corners of the world in their insatiable appetite for new knowledge of the past, the Victorians excavated and collected avidly for the newly created museums. Those artefacts that could not be fitted into the museums were amassed in their homes and if the genuine articles were too expensive, they copied and embellished them.

By the 1840s technical and industrial growth had created an enormous level of output so that the availability of goods was high. The need, some would say, the greed, of the Victorians to ornament their homes, coupled with the 'collector' craze saw homes bursting at the seams with possessions. Understandably, certain sections of society expressed concern with this materialistic drive. Among such people was the artistic elite whose belief was that the general standard of design and good taste of the nation needed to be raised, not by an ever increasing quantity, but by a return to the appreciation of quality.

It was with this in mind that the Great Exhibition of 1851 was conceived. Unfortunately, along its path the plan backfired and its eventual manifestation was one of ostentatious vulgarity; the primary aim and objective of displaying and re-educating the masses back into good design lost in a sea of showiness. Queen Victoria thought it, "quite the effect of fairyland", but Owen Jones, "a fruitless struggle after novelty, irrespective of fitness".

However, the striving after good design principles had been quietly carrying on in other areas prior to the Great Exhibition. In 1836, the Art Union of London had been set up, where members, by way of a lottery, could win works of art as prizes and in 1840 government grants were given for the establishment of design schools in Glasgow, Birmingham, Manchester, Paisley and Leeds.

Artists dictated taste in design through their work in the public buildings sector. The influence of men such as A. W. N. Pugin, William Morris, Owen Jones, John Ruskin, Prince Albert and Henry Cole was paramount. Indeed Henry Cole (who founded the Victoria & Albert Museum in London) undertook in 1849 the commissioning of artists to design simple, everyday glass, silver and ceramics. He subsequently started a factory in order to produce the designs.

Pugin and Morris are perhaps the two most important and influential designers of the era, brilliant and prolific in many areas of Victorian style as they were. Pugin, a Roman Catholic convert, considered medieval Christianity to have been the most pure form of worship and the age was therefore (Christianity being the source dictating all spheres of life) one to be emulated in all its facets, particularly architectural. Henry Cole and his followers - the new Gothic Revivalists, comprising architects, glass painters, and furniture designers - worked closely together on the major expansion of civic and church building of the time, rejecting the cool 'pagan' Regency classicism in favour of the devout medieval, Gothic style of romanticism.

This fascination with the past, coupled with the pride in and approbation of industrial development is an interesting mixture. Perhaps the surge forward towards greater and greater mechanization was unsettling and therefore the desire to revisit the past was actually a search for stability in an age of overwhelming changes.

An influx of continental artists to Britain escaping the turmoils of 1848 and 1870, who brought with them rescued objects d'art and their own design styles, added another factor to Victorian design style. Designers like Pugin incorporated fragments of medieval carvings and panelling into reproductions of European styles producing an ornate and grandiose style. Pugin's tour de force, the Palace of Westminster in London, shows him at his Gothic best.

It is amidst this elaborate style during the second half of the century that anti-industrialist and socialist William Morris arrived, cutting a swathe through the fussiness and preaching a return to traditional crafts and standards. He viewed the machine as an enslaver of the working classes. His design philosophy, based on simple lines and a correspondingly simple way of life, was also prompted by the medieval period in which he saw, not Pugin's ideal of spiritual purity, but rather the honesty and integrity of design for functional use. He helped to blur the line between fine and applied arts and his admirers and sympathizers, such as Crane, Day, Benson and Mackmurdo, helped establish this new school of thought through the Arts and Crafts Exhibition Society, the Century Guild, the Art Workers Guild and the Guild of Handicraft.

The simpler approach, particularly of people like Nesfield, Goodwin

◆ Furniture designed by A.W.N. Pugin in about 1840 for the drawing room at Eastnor Castle in Herefordshire matches the elaborately ornate style of the decoration.

11

and Shaw with their designs of clean lines and their attention to materials, lead to what is termed the English Domestic Revival and subsequently, by the turn of the century, to Art Nouveau, a direct outcome of the Arts and Crafts Movement, heralding designers such as Tiffany, Lalique, Gallé and Brangwyn.

We are extremely lucky, today, that we can still view the Victorian style at first hand. A walk through many of our cities will bring us into contact with Victorian-built properties and because of the vast amount of goods produced many of us will have items dating from this period in our homes today.

Inevitably the design styles had an influence on embroidery and tapestry work. Pugin encouraged the revival of ecclesiastical needlework. Societies were formed to encourage this, the vestments being designed by various architects and executed in medieval applied techniques. Morris orchestrated the revival of secular artistry, exploring the old techniques of crewel work together with his family and producing hangings and coverlets with fluid foliage designs and medieval-inspired subjects.

The legacy of needlework that we have from this period falls into two categories. The examples of decorated furnishings as bought or worked by the wealthier section of society for their homes or for personal use and the samplers worked mostly by children.

The charity schools and orphanages where the poorer children were given a very basic education, taught spinning, knitting and sewing, in the hope that some of their pupils would eventually be able to eke out a living caring for the linen and clothing of the more wealthy. The Victorians were obsessed with marking every item of clothing or linen and this accounts for the dense practice samplers, showing line upon line of initials, numbers and small patterns. More often than not they were worked in one colour on linen or coarse-meshed canvas using wool and were signed with the name of the stitcher, date and place of stitching (see page 85). They often included a pious verse to express the stitcher's humility. The sombreness of the Victorians is evident in the samplers which contain lengthy biblical verses with hardly any light relief by way of pretty motifs.

Samplers were produced with decorative borders and embellishment, however, and whereas they did not use as many different motifs as their predecessors, they had a balance and symmetry which in itself is quite soothing to the eye. Traditional motifs were still used, including some dating back to the 17th century, and houses were increasingly featured. The greater simplicity of motif shape was in contrast to the ornate Berlin woolwork (discussed in greater detail on page 36) which became so popular from the 1840s onwards and which was to be found in great profusion in Victorian homes.

By the end of the century some children's samplers featured Berlin woolwork styles mixed together with the more traditional motifs. Samplers were usually worked in cross stitch but Berlin woolwork generally involved a wide variety of stitches.

Across Europe samplers continued to be embroidered during this period. Dutch sampler work is distinguished by the more random placing of motifs with little use of religious text. Usually dated and named, the samplers were generally wider than they were long with a mass of diverse motifs ranging from all things secular to ecclesiastical. The Germans favoured highly ornate, Gothic-style alphabets with short religious inscriptions, and motifs depicting domestic items, animals and village scenes, all worked in a wide range of colours. Interestingly, they obviously considered their work as something to be treasured and often edged the embroidery with ruched silk ribbon or braid. Lace-work and cut work seem to have been the chosen styles of the Italians who produced beautifully intricate, fine designs, while the French worked their embroidery on fine muslin without moral texts or verses, so that for the rest of Europe the sampler was still most probably produced as vocational practice for the embellishment of ecclesiastical garments or the fashion world rather than as a piece of design in its own right.

North America's love affair with the sampler was no doubt fuelled by the large number of emigrants to the New World and similarities between their samplers and the various European styles can be found. Where large groups of Dutch or German émigrés had settled the styles remained more akin to those of their country of origin. This can be seen particularly in samplers from the Pennsylvania area worked at this time. However, the new Americans were also developing their own unique style. Much less formal than the British counterparts, their samplers were generally worked on a flax/wool mixture using silk or wool, were more pictorial in content and showed an increasing republicanism with the frequent appearance of spreadwinged eagles among the stitched motifs. Genealogical samplers with stitched family trees or tables of family generations enjoyed a popularity and, although not particularly attractive, they provide an interesting insight into the sociological history of the time.

The legacy of needlework and in particular, sampler work, worldwide that is available from this time is enormous and it is impossible to discuss it in great depth or to cover all areas in a general introduction to the period. Hopefully, however, I have provided enough of an outline to whet your appetite for more information about this fascinating time in design history and to put in context those future heirlooms which you are about to stitch!

◆ A marvellous example of a schoolgirl's work containing three alphabets, one highly decorative and the two others an elegant upper and lower case script. It was worked by one Marie Brehm as a memento of her schooling.

Floral Alphabet Sampler

Perhaps best known as the author of 'The Grammar of Ornament' (1856), Owen Jones was trained as an architect but became far more successful as a commentator on style and design. His book was, and still is, considered an invaluable source of inspiration for designers. Its cavalcade of patterns from all civilizations and cultures is typical of the eclectic approach to design of the Victorians. Jones also formed his own philosophy regarding design principles. Some of these were drawn from Pugin, one of the most famous of the Victorian Gothic architects, and are also echoed by the Arts and Craft Movement. Owen suggested that, "as architecture, so all works of the Decorative Arts should possess fitness, proportion, harmony, the result of which is repose".

Designed by Jones in about 1852 and entitled 'Floral Pattern' (see page 16), it is this wallpaper pattern which provides the basis for the border of the alphabet sampler. It is a relatively easy border to work and the petal shades could easily be changed to suit your own room scheme.

The corner motifs are from part of an English stoneware toilet service, as shown in 'The Silber and Fleming Glass and China Book'. Such publications were common during the Victorian age and were the forerunners of our direct mail catalogues. They were produced by manufacturers, importers or agents and much consulted by the middle classes in their insatiable quest for possessions. Many reproductions of such catalogues are now available and are a wonderful insight into Victorian domestic life, offering everything from photo frames to street lights, cruets to chandeliers.

The cartouches, butterflies and lilies are all motifs from samplers held in the Netherlands Open Air Museum at Arnhem, Holland. The Dutch have a strong tradition of sampler embroidery and there is no doubt that they helped to establish the same love of the work in North America when many emigrated to the New World during the second half of the 19th century. Their endearing motifs and accompanying symbolism have also found a special place in British embroidery work.

The alphabet is taken from a Victorian schoolgirl's sampler (see page 17).

◆ Below: The illustrations in the Victorian equivalent of the mail-order catalogue are hand-drawn and make decorative objects in themselves, as well as providing contemporary motifs.

Right: The Floral Alphabet Sampler takes its letters from a piece of period stitching and its border from motifs printed on wallpaper and stoneware of the same time.

STONEWARE.

3321

MATERIALS

*1 piece of cream or white Aida, 18 count,
21 x 24 in (54 x 60 cm)*

tapestry needle(s), size 26

lightweight wadding for mounting (optional)

*1 skein each of stranded cotton in the
following shades:*

		DMC	Anchor
	dusty blue	334	977
	dark sea blue	824	164
	antique green	3052	859
	pale brick red	760	9
	brick red	3328	10
	new maroon	3802	897
	pale mauve	210	108
	buff	945	881
	green-gold	833	907
	medium brown	3772	914

2 skeins of stranded cotton in:

	dark grey-green	501	878

*Finished size of design: 15 ½ x 17 ½ in
(38.5 x 44.5 cm)*

METHOD

As this is a heavily-worked piece, I recommend that you hem or tack the raw edges of the fabric before starting to cross stitch, in order to prevent fraying (see page 90).

Fold the fabric in half lengthwise to find the centre vertical line and mark with a line of tacking stitches. Now measure down this fold for 3 in (7.5 cm) from the top of the fabric. This will give the point at which you start stitching on the fabric. Find the starting stitch marked on the chart on page 18 and begin work on the fabric with this stitch.

Work in cross stitch using two strands of cotton over one thread intersection.

Work the top line of the floral border, then the side borders. Next stitch the internal design working in bands across the fabric, starting at

◆ Right: Block-printed wallpaper with
a distinctive design by Owen Jones
is the inspiration for the sampler
border.

the top with the alphabet and aligning the motifs carefully. Use the centre vertical line to place the large motif and finally work the lower case alphabet. Once the internal design has all been stitched, enclose the work by stitching the lower border.

When the stitching is complete, wash if necessary and press gently from the wrong side (see page 90). For finishing and mounting instructions, see page 92.

◆ Above: A sampler stitched by a ten-year-old schoolgirl in 1834, probably to help her learn her letters, gives us a very useful upper and lower case alphabet.

MATERIALS

*1 piece of cream Aida, 16 count, 9 x 16 in
(23 x 40 cm)*

tapestry needle, size 26

*1 piece of iron-on interfacing, same size as
Aida*

*1 pair of 6 in (15 cm) bell pull ends or two
pieces of ½ in /15 mm doweling and hanging
ribbon*

*1 skein each of stranded cotton in the
following shades:*

		DMC	Anchor
▨	sea blue	826	161
▨	pale sea blue	827	9159
▨	med. antique pink	3726	970
▨	light antique pink	3727	969

*Finished size of design: 4 ⅝ x 10 ¼ in
(12 x 26 cm)*

Welcome Wallhanging

The stylized floral motif decorating the 'welcome' message is taken from a sampler stitched in 1834 and now held in Jean Elliot's marvellous collection (see page 17). The embroidery in the photograph has my initials for which, obviously, you would substitute your own. The initials could be followed by the name of your home or this could be stitched in place of your initials. If you wish to add your house name allow a further 3 inches (7.5 cm) to the fabric length and space the name two squares above or below your initials. This would make a longer piece which could be displayed as a bell pull.

METHOD

Fold the fabric in half lengthwise to find the centre vertical line. Crease lightly. Measure 3 in (7.5 cm) down this centre line from the top of the fabric. This places the centre starting stitch on the fabric, as marked on the chart on page 24.

Work in cross stitch using two strands of cotton over one thread intersection. If adding a house name, use the alphabet on pages 18 to 19 and follow the instructions on letter spacing given on page 92.

When the stitching is complete, wash if necessary and press gently from the wrong side (see page 90). Turn under a hem equally on each of the long sides, to make a 6 in (15 cm) completed width. Leave at least 1 in (2.5 cm) of unworked fabric above and below the stitching and form the rest of the fabric into a deep hem left open at the sides to take the bell pull ends. Trim the interfacing to fit inside the hems at the back of the work, then iron it in position. Insert the bell pull ends or doweling and hanging ribbon.

◆ **Far right: This hanging would fit well in a Victorian home where framed mottoes and sayings were popular wall decorations.**

HOME
SWEET
HOME

AVW 1995

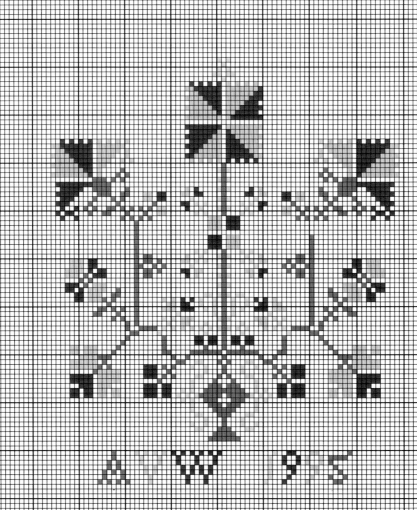

Napkin

Having stitched the Floral Alphabet Sampler and hung it in your dining room, perhaps you would now like to complement the work by stitching a set of napkins, using the same border motifs inspired by Owen Jones' wallpaper and the Victorian crockery design. All the large samplers in this book contain a host of possibilities for isolating and adapting patterns. This project simply repeats a design, others, like the wall-hanging on page 23, take part of one pattern and incorporate it with motifs from a different source.

METHOD

Count thirteen threads up from the fray-stop line of stitching at the bottom of the napkin and twelve threads in from the stitching line at the righthand side. Begin work at this point following the starting stitch marked on the chart on page 26.

Work in cross stitch using two strands of cotton over two thread intersections.

When the stitching is complete, rinse if necessary and press the fabric gently from the wrong side.

MATERIALS

1 set of 4 cream or white Sal-Em napkins (see page 93 for stockist)

tapestry needle(s), 24 or 26

1 skein each of stranded cotton in the following shades:

		DMC	Anchor
■	*dark grey-green*	*501*	*878*
▨	*pale green-gold*	*834*	*874*
▨	*antique green*	*3052*	*859*
▨	*pale dusty rose*	*3354*	*74*
▨	*dusty rose*	*3731*	*38*

Finished size of design: 7 1/4 x 2 3/4 in (18.5 x 7 cm)

◆ An embroidered napkin makes an elegant table decoration.

Jewelled Cross Sampler

Mainstream fashion in the 1830s was typified by dropped waists, highly corseted figures, boat necklines, huge leg-of-mutton or puff sleeves and full-petticoated, flounced skirts which culminated in 1842 in the famous crinoline style. Jewellery design mirrored this fussiness and fullness of dress and the low necklines and tight cuffs set off necklaces and bracelets perfectly. Jewellery was an important item of dress for the Victorians with different types being considered appropriate for the day or for the evening and there was even special mourning wear. Hair ornaments, earrings and brooches were produced in great profusion in a wide range of colours created by all kinds of gemstones.

The standard of design and craftsmanship of all types was quite superb and these pieces remain rightfully popular and in demand to this day. The settings were often as important to the design as the value of the inset stones. The designs were eclectic, mirroring the free style of the period. Gold with semi-precious stones was used, as in the Gothic style cross opposite, and the east was a strong influence, as can be seen in the necklace with its enamelled designs of birds, flowers and insects. These pieces have inspired the sampler design made in the shape of a cross, which in itself was an extremely popular item of Victorian jewellery.

The border is made up of a repeat motif taken from a small detail on a French sampler.

◆ Above: A gold cross with quatrefoil ends set with emeralds and sapphires and with a central ruby, gives the outline for the sampler.
Left: The Japanese-style birds, flowers and insects of this gold and enamel necklace have inspired the motifs. It was designed in France in about 1869.

27

METHOD

This, like all the samplers, is a detailed project which will take some time to complete, so I recommend that you hem or tack the raw edges of the fabric before starting to cross stitch, to prevent fraying (see page 90). Do this after you have positioned the starting stitch.

Fold the fabric in half lengthwise to find the centre vertical line and crease lightly. Now measure down this fold for 3 in (7.5 cm) from the top of the fabric. This will give the point at which you start stitching on the fabric. Find the starting stitch marked on the chart on page 30 and begin work on the fabric with this stitch.

Use two strands of cotton, working over one thread intersection. Work the outlines in back stitch and the rest in cross stitch.

Work the border first, then stitch the outline of the cross, ensuring that it is symmetrically placed within the border. Next stitch the motifs within the cross. Finally fill in the background of the cross with the chequered pattern of cross stitches.

When the stitching is complete, wash if necessary and press gently from the wrong side (see page 90). For finishing and mounting instructions, see page 92.

MATERIALS

*1 piece of cream Aida, 16 count,
16½ x 20 in (42 x 51 cm)*

tapestry needle, size 26

lightweight wadding for mounting (optional)

1 skein each of stranded cotton in the following shades:

		DMC	Anchor
	dark orange	721	324
	new medium green	3815	216
	pale green	368	214
	new dark turquoise	3808	675
	green-gold	833	907
	dark sea blue	824	164
	light sea blue	813	160
	wine red	816	44
	dark red	321	9046
	dark grey	413	401
	pale gold	726	295
	very deep pink	961	76
	deep pink	962	75
	blush pink	963	73
	pale mauve	210	108
	deep purple	327	100
	peach	352	9

backstitch border of cross

	pale green-gold	834	874

2 skeins of stranded cotton in:

	pale grey-green	504	875

Finished size of design: 10¼ x 14½ in (26 x 37 cm)

◆ **Left: A little motif from a French sampler stitched in 1893 gives the outer border design for the Jewelled Cross Sampler (far left).**

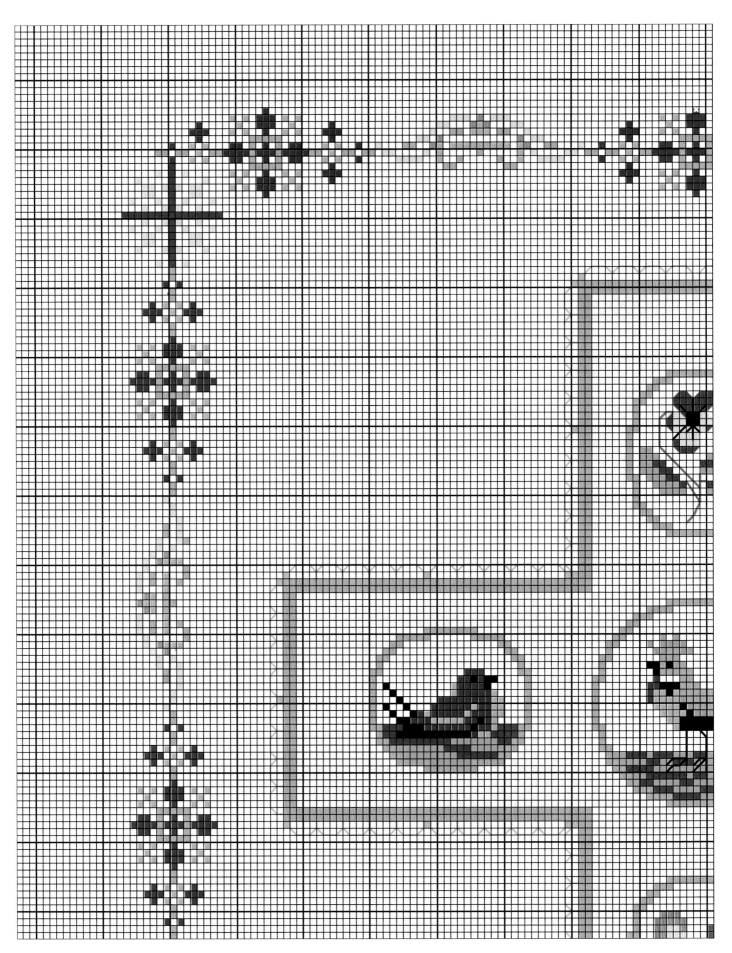

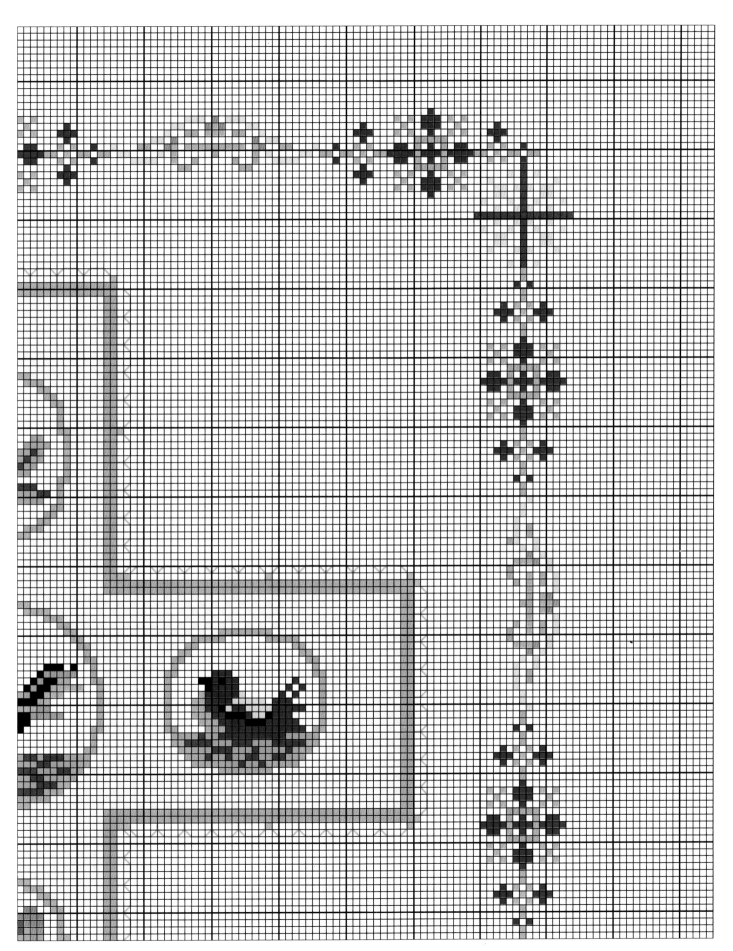

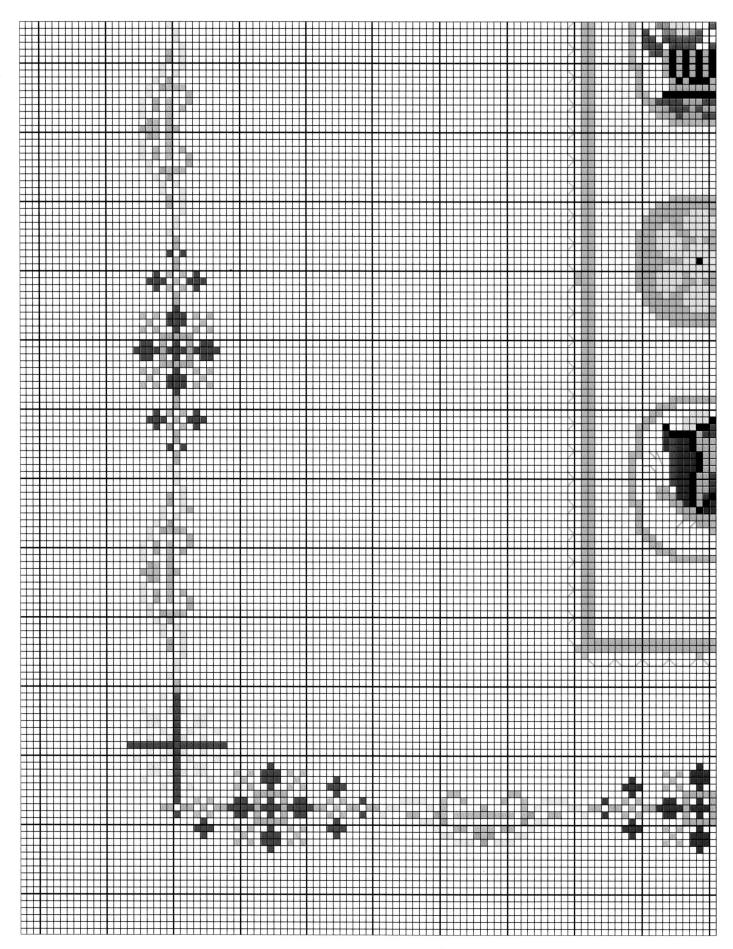

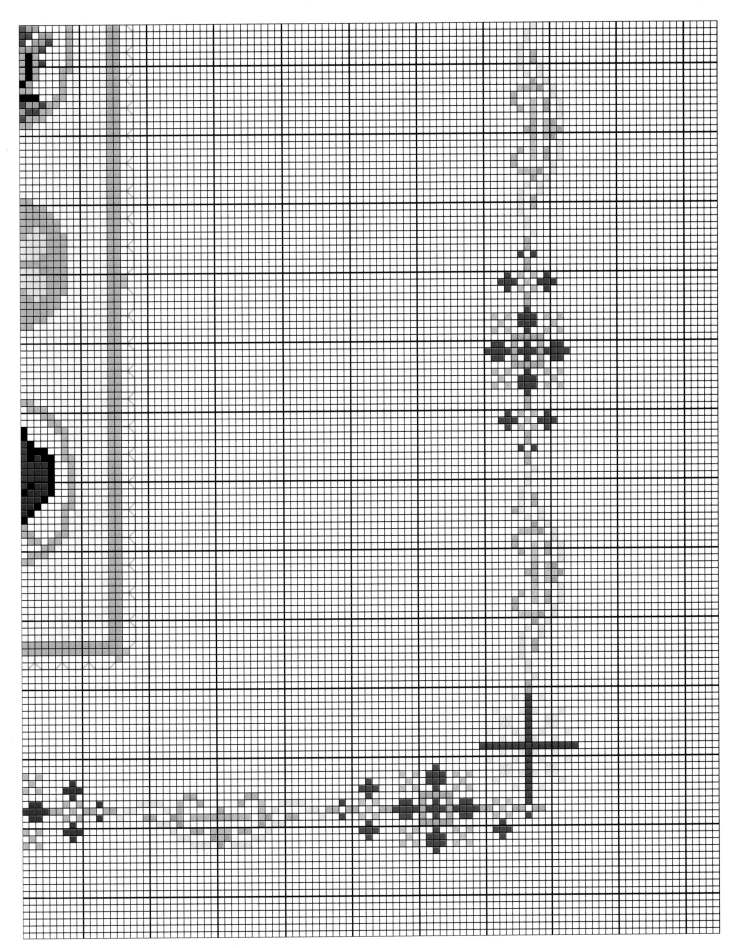

MATERIALS

*1 piece of white Aida, 22 count, 3 x 3 in
(7.5 x 7.5 cm), for the brooch*

tapestry needle, size 26

*1 brooch, silver edged and oval, 1 ½ x 2 in
(4 x 5 cm) in diameter (see page 93 for
stockist)*

*1 skein each of stranded cotton in the
following shades:*

		DMC	Anchor
▨	deep purple	327	100
▨	pale green	368	214
■	dark grey	413	401
▨	new medium green	3815	216
▭	pale gold	726	295

*Finished size of design: ¾ x ⅞ in
(2 x 2.3 cm)*

Brooch

This and the following project take small motifs from the Jewelled Cross Sampler (page 28) and show how they can be used effectively on smaller pieces. The violet motif is particularly attractive when delicately worked on 22 count fabric and mounted in a brooch. The Victorian ladies were very fond of brooches and wore them for both day and evening decoration. This is a useful little flower motif to add to your pattern library.

METHOD

Fold the fabric in half lengthwise and crosswise to find the centre point. Crease lightly. Start work at this point following the centre stitch of the motif on the chart on pages 30 to 31.

Work in cross stitch and back stitch using one strand of cotton over one thread intersection.

When the stitching is complete, wash if necessary and press gently from the wrong side (see page 90). Trim and mount the piece following the manufacturer's instructions.

◆ Right: This delicate little brooch presents another working of the violet motif from the Jewelled Cross Sampler (page 28), this time on a much finer fabric.

Baby's Bib and Towel

Alternative uses for two of the small motifs on the Jewelled Cross Sampler are demonstrated on a little bib and towel, designed to be pretty and useful pieces for a newborn baby.

METHOD

To make the bib, fold the fabric in half lengthwise and crosswise to establish the centre point. Crease lightly. Count eight squares to the left of this point and start stitching following the marked square on the chart below. Work in cross stitch using three strands of cotton over one thread

intersection. Reverse the right-hand motif.

To make the towel, fold the flatweave band in half lengthwise and crosswise to find the centre point. Count eight squares to the left of this point and start stitching following the marked square on the chart below. Work in cross stitch as above. Stitch one complete motif, then continue stitching motifs on either side until the band is filled.

MATERIALS

1 towel, with 14 count evenweave band
1 round Aida bib, 14 count
tapestry needle, size 24
1 skein each of stranded cotton in the following shades:

		DMC	Anchor
■	grey	317	400
▨	red-brown	355	341
▨	yellow	743	305
▨	blue	798	131
▨	pale blue	809	130
■	wine red	816	44

Finished size of design (single motif):
3 ¼ x 1 in (6.5 x 2.5 cm)

◆ Left: Two further uses of the duck motifs from page 28 shown in different combinations on baby linen.

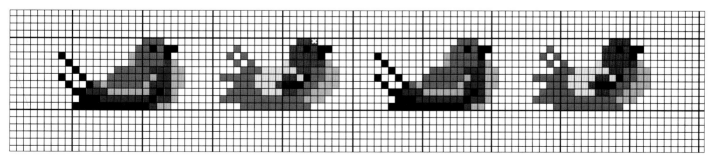

Bargello Sampler

The border for this project is taken from one of many patterns featured on a Berlin woolwork sampler held in the Victoria & Albert Museum in London. This lovely bargello pattern cries out to be used as a border. A traditional design since Renaissance times, it is used here to surround a posy of flowers inspired by another sampler in Jean Elliot's collection (see page 93). The original flowers are presented in muted shades and follow the Berlin woolwork style of floral design.

Berlin woolwork gained its name and subsequent enormous popularity during the 1830s, from the German city of its origin. Its success was due mainly to a combination of three factors: the introduction of chemical dyes, a new type of wool and colour pattern charts. The aniline dyes produced even brighter shades and the wools were finer. The squared paper patterns produced for the first time in colour were easy to follow and gave the needleworker a more realistic representation of the motifs using shading and more natural shapes. Berlin woolwork reached the peak of its popularity during the 1880s. It was used both for sampler work and for the decoration of all kinds of household goods, shoes and handbags. Samplers featured biblical scenes, well-known paintings, children and animals but were mostly floral.

Strip samplers, such as the one featured here, were often executed by professional needlewomen and echo the original intention of the band samplers of previous times; that of demonstrating skill levels, either to show clients for commissioned work or to be sold in the new specialist shops for amateurs to copy. A variety of stitches were used: Florentine, Hungarian, cross and satin, as well as couched and laid work.

The influence of Berlin woolwork on children's sampler work towards the end of the century can be seen in the growing number of floral sprays in their pieces and is therefore a useful fact when trying to date an unsigned sampler.

◆ Below: The intricately stitched bouquet of flowers from this mid 19th century sampler forms the centrepiece of the Bargello sampler.
Far right: This sampler combines two traditional embroidery styles to produce a striking piece for a modern needleworker.

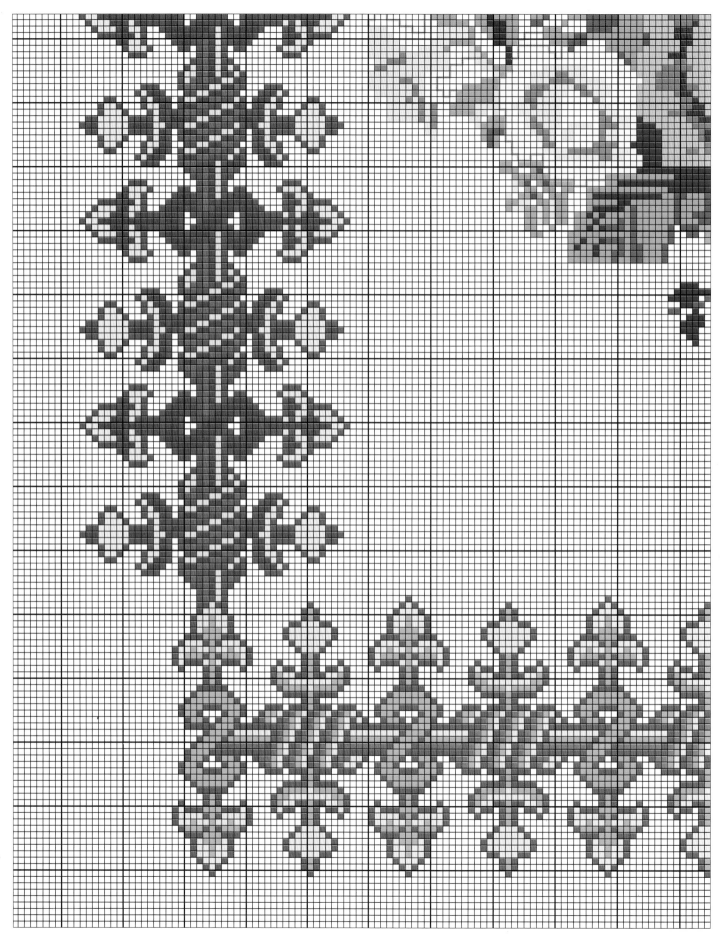

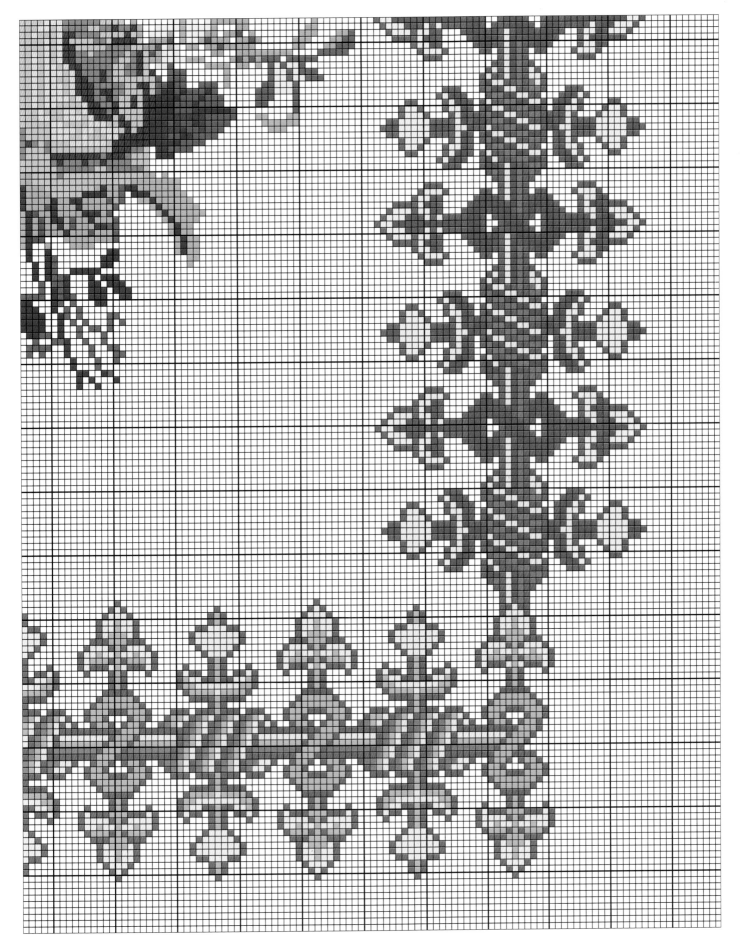

MATERIALS

1 piece of white Belfast linen, 28 count,
25 x 21 in (62 x 53 cm)

tapestry needle(s), size 26

lightweight wadding for mounting (optional)

1 skein each of stranded cotton in the
following shades:

		DMC	Anchor
flowers			
	dark green	319	217
	green	367	216
	pale green	368	214
	very pale green	369	213
	light gold	as border	
	pale orange	742	303
	yellow	743	305
	light yellow	744	301
	blue	798	131
	pale blue	809	130
	maroon	3685	69
	light maroon	as border	
	dusky pink	3688	66
	pale dusky pink	3689	49
	medium brown	as border	
	light orange-brown	921	338
border			
	light maroon	3687	68

2 skeins of stranded cotton in:

	pale khaki	472	278

3 skeins of stranded cotton in:

	medium brown	3772	914
	light gold	725	306

4 skeins of stranded cotton in:

	sea blue	826	161

Finished size of design: 18 1/2 x 14 1/2 in
(47 x 37.5 cm)

◆ **Right: This woolwork sampler from the mid 19th century might well have been stitched by a professional embroiderer as a display piece to show the available patterns.**

METHOD

As this is a detailed project that will take some time to complete, I strongly recommend that you hem or tack the raw edges of the fabric before starting to cross stitch, to prevent fraying (see page 90).

Fold the fabric in half lengthwise and crosswise, then mark these lines with tacking stitches. This will mark the centre point at which you start stitching on the fabric. Find the starting stitch marked on the chart on page 38 and begin work on the fabric with this stitch.

Use two strands of cotton, working over two thread intersections. Work in cross stitch throughout. Work outwards from the starting stitch, completing the flower motifs before working the border. It is a good idea to stitch each flower completely before moving on to the next. Although this will involve more colour changes in the needle, it will help with the positioning. Try working with several needles (see page 91). When stitching the border, fill in each twist with the specified colours before moving on to the next bargello pattern. This will give you a double check that you have followed the main shade placement correctly.

When the stitching is complete, wash if necessary and press gently from the wrong side (see page 90). For finishing and mounting instructions, see page 92.

Workbox

What better way to store all your cross stitch materials than in this elegant workbox? Using the flower bouquet which forms the centrepiece of the Bargello Sampler and worked on 28 count fabric, this embroidery would enhance any room and make a splendid gift. It could also be worked as a piece for a pole screen with the addition of one or more of the borders given in various projects throughout the book. Berlin wool-work pole screens and firescreens were popular display pieces in Victorian homes.

METHOD

Fold the fabric in half lengthwise and crosswise to find the centre point. Crease lightly. Start work at this point following the stitch marked on the chart on page 38.

Work in cross stitch using two strands of cotton over two thread intersections.

When the stitching is complete, wash if necessary and press gently from the wrong side (see page 90). Trim and mount the piece following the manufacturer's instructions.

MATERIALS

1 piece of white or ivory linen, 28 count, 15 x 13 in (38 x 33 cm)

tapestry needle(s), size 24 or 26

1 small workbox (see page 93 for stockist)

1 skein each of stranded cotton in the following shades:

		DMC	Anchor
	dark green	319	217
	green	367	216
	pale green	368	214
	very pale green	369	213
	light gold	725	306
	pale orange	742	303
	yellow	743	305
	light yellow	744	301
	blue	798	131
	pale blue	809	130
	light orange-brown	921	338
	maroon	3685	69
	light maroon	3687	68
	dusky pink	3688	66
	pale dusky pink	3689	49
	medium brown	3772	914

Finished size of design: 7 ¾ x 7 ⅓ in (19.5 x 19 cm)

◆ **Left: The bouquet of flowers from the Bargello Sampler (page 37) is given pride of place on the lid of this workbox.**

Forget-me-not Pot

This spray of rose buds and forget-me-nots has been put together from part of the design which provided the floral bouquet for the centre of the Bargello Sampler (page 37).

It is a useful motif for your collection, which is shown here as a decoration on a pretty crystal pot, but could equally well be used on a smaller count of fabric and mounted in a greetings card. The sampler also has a charming border just waiting to be used.

METHOD

Fold the fabric in half lengthwise and crosswise to find the centre point. Crease lightly. Start work at this point following the stitch marked on the chart on page 45.

Work in cross stitch using two strands of cotton over one thread intersection.

When the stitching is complete, press the fabric gently from the wrong side. Place the interfacing centrally on the reverse of the work and iron in position. Trim and mount the piece in the pot lid following the manufacturer's instructions.

◆ The delicate little design on this pot lid is perfectly complemented by the crystal base.

MATERIALS

1 piece of Aida fabric, 22 count, 6 x 6 in (15 x 15 cm)

1 crystal pot, 3 ½ in (9 cm) diameter lid (see page 93 for stockist)

1 piece of iron-on interfacing, same size as Aida

tapestry needle, size 26

1 skein each of stranded cotton in the following shades:

		DMC	Anchor
	very pale green	369	213
	pale dusty pink	3689	49
	dusky pink	3688	66
	light maroon	3687	68
	maroon	3685	69
	pale green	368	214
	dark green	319	217
	pale blue	809	130
	blue	798	131
	green	367	216
	medium brown	3772	914

Finished size of design: 2½ x 2¾ in (6.5 x 7 cm)

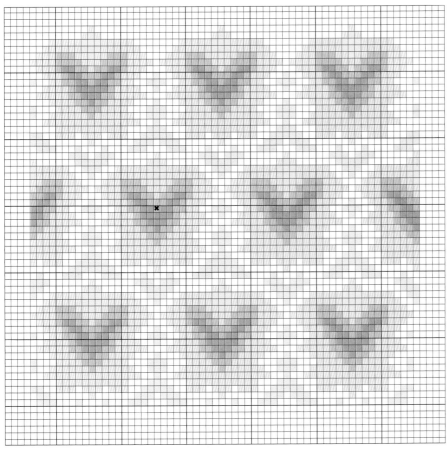

Top: Forget-me-not pot
Left: Tray

MATERIALS

*1 piece of white Aida, 14 count, 11 x 11 in
(28 x 28 cm)*

tapestry needle, size 24

*1 piece of iron-on interfacing, same size as
Aida*

1 tray base (see page 93 for stockist)

*1 skein each of stranded cotton in the
following shades:*

		DMC	Anchor
	peach	352	9
	pale peach	353	6
	very pale peach	754	4146
	very pale green	369	213

*Finished size of design illustrated:
6 ½ x 6 ½ in (16.5 x 16.5 cm)*

Tray

The photographs of the sources of inspiration can themselves provide further scope for pattern adaptation. This tray pattern has been taken from the same 19th century woolwork sampler which produced the border for the Bargello Sampler (see page 42). This motif makes an effective all-over cover design for a tray: alternative uses could be for a dressing table set in pastel shades or for a workbox top. The pattern is easily reduced or expanded to the required size for the chosen mount by adding or subtracting the linking motifs. A simple double line of cross stitches will give a sharp, clean edge to the design if required.

METHOD

Fold the fabric in half lengthwise and crosswise to find the centre point. Crease lightly. Find the centre point of one of the motifs on the chart on page 45 and, starting with this stitch, work the complete motif. Work in cross stitch using two strands of cotton over one thread intersection. Repeat the motif as necessary to fill the required design area. Lastly, fill in the linking designs.

When the stitching is complete, press the fabric gently from the wrong side. Place the interfacing centrally on the reverse of the work and iron in position. Trim and place the fabric centrally in the mount following the manufacturer's instructions.

◆ **Right: A useful all-over design makes
an effective decoration for this
practical drinks tray.**

Berlin Woolwork Sampler

A beautiful interlace of flowers forms the border of this sampler. It is inspired by part of a Berlin woolwork design (see page 36) of circa 1850, which was originally worked as a chair back and can be viewed at the Victoria & Albert Museum in London.

This commemorative sampler is designed to be adaptable to many different events, having space for names or a piece of poetry. It is worked on white fabric here but the flowers would look equally dramatic on a dark background as in the original source. If the colours are a little bright for your taste they could be easily toned down, but be careful not to unbalance the design as some of the flowerheads could easily dominate the work due to their size. Might I suggest that, having chosen your shades and grouped the sample colours together, you then extract the main flowerhead shades and take them down in intensity by one shade.

METHOD

Measure 4 in (10 cm) down from the top right corner of the fabric and 4 in (10 cm) in from the righthand side, and begin stitching at this point following the point marked on the chart on page 49.

Work in cross stitch using two strands of cotton over one thread intersection.

From the starting stitch, work down the border line and along the base, then begin stitching the flowers. Work each leaf or flower head completely before starting the next. This will help to avoid miscalculations. Personalize your work by using the alphabet shown in the sampler on page 15, placing the letters centrally using the method described on page 92.

When the stitching is complete, wash if necessary and press gently from the wrong side (see page 90). For finishing and mounting instructions, see page 92.

MATERIALS

1 piece of white fabric, 16 count, 15 x 19 in (38 x 47 cm)

tapestry needles, size 24/26

lightweight wadding for mounting (optional)

1 skein each of stranded cotton in the following shades:

		DMC	Anchor
	light rust	350	11
	rust	817	19
	peach	352	9
	pale brown	407	91
	light brown	632	936
	dark brown	839	360
	very dark brown	938	381
	silver brown	840	379
	medium beige	437	362
	fawn	676	89
	light fawn	677	300
	beige	738	361
	yellow	743	305
	very dark green	890	683
	dark antique green	3051	861
	antique green	3052	859
	pale antique green	3053	858
	blue	798	131
	very pale blue	800	144
	pale blue	809	130
	very dark blue	820	134

Finished size of design: 9 x 12¼ in (22.5 cm x 31.5 cm)

◆ **Above: The vibrant colours and realistic flower designs on this chair-back are typical of Berlin woolwork. Part of the design makes a striking border for the commemorative sampler shown overleaf.**

Symbolic Spot Sampler

Sourced from many samplers, Dutch, Welsh, Scottish and English, this project presents a selection of traditional motifs framed within a border typical of the period.

By the 19th century cross stitch had become the mainstay stitch of sampler work. Most samplers now had a border, most commonly of carnations or strawberries, enclosing the traditional motifs of flowers, animals and birds together with great statements in verse expounding the virtues of humility or the consequences of sin or the inevitability of one's mortality.

Morbid rhymes abounded among the pretty motifs. It seems the Victorians allowed a little frivolity and lightness only if accompanied by a sombre, restraining thought. I have not included any of these epithets as most are rather depressing and I do not relish the image of children sitting crouched over their work diligently stitching about their own mortality!

Although some motifs were embroidered purely for aesthetic reasons, others were included because of the symbolism attached to them and in the light of this tradition, I have chosen or adapted patterns for this sampler, that through the stitching will wish the recipients well.

The borders are completely decorative and are taken from M. A. Tipper's sampler of 1868 (see page 57) which can be viewed at the Fitzwilliam Museum in Cambridge. Three patterns are shown demonstrating how easily different patterns can be successfully linked.

The tree of life at the centre of this sampler, the stags, crowns and birds are taken from a sampler worked by Anne Thomas which can be viewed at St Fagan's Museum in Wales.

The tree of life was an important symbol, commonly found on European (particularly British and Dutch) sampler work from the middle of the 18th century, though we can trace the importance of the symbol as far back as the Ancient World. It is often flanked by human figures, animals or roosting birds and represents the bearer and renewer of life. By working the motif onto a dedicated sampler we are wishing the recipient a long, fruitful, excellent life. Fruit trees are also used in similar fashion.

◆ Above: A young Victorian's alphabet sampler with some intriguing sets of initials. The bowl of apples provides one of the symbols for the modern spot sampler overleaf.

The crowns are symbols of eternity and the stags represent gentleness, the tulip head, perfect love, and the flower-filled vase, the source of life (see page 58).

The final motif, a bowl of fruit, particularly apples, is a symbol of fertility and love. The pattern used here is taken from the Jane Ann Rutherford sampler of 1859, in a private collection (see page 93).

The sampler would commemorate a child's birth or a marriage equally well as the motifs and their symbolism are appropriate to either event.

MATERIALS

1 piece cream or white Aida, 14 count, 20 x 22 in (51 x 56 cm)

tapestry needle(s), size 24

lightweight wadding for mounting (optional)

1 skein each of stranded cotton in the following shades;

		DMC	Anchor
	medium rose pink	335	41
	pale khaki	471	265
	sea blue	826	161
	dark green-gold	832	907
	pale rose pink	3326	36
	v. pale red brown	3779	868
	new pale gold	3822	305
	new brown	3826	349
	new copper	3828	888
	dark grey-green	501	878

2 skeins of stranded cotton in:

	dark khaki	469	267

Finished size of design: 12 ½ x 14 ⅝ in (32 x 37 cm)

METHOD

As on the previous samplers, I recommend that you hem or tack the raw edges of the fabric before starting to cross stitch, in order to prevent fraying (see page 90).

Fold the fabric in half lengthwise and crosswise, then mark these lines with tacking stitches. This will mark the centre point at which you start stitching on the fabric. Find the starting stitch marked on the chart on page 54 and begin work on the fabric with this stitch.

Use three strands of cotton, working over one thread intersection. Work in cross stitch throughout.

Stitch the top horizontal part of the border first, then the two sides. Next start stitching the internal motifs, beginning with the trees in the upper corners. Now chart out the name or verse you wish to stitch, following the instructions for letter spacing given on page 92 and using the alphabet from pages 18 to 19. Stitch the letters, then surround them with the internal motif shown on the chart, shortening or lengthening it as necessary. Work the surround, then the tree of life and the other motifs. If you had to extend the name surround, you may wish to reposition the flower-filled vase motif to sit centrally in the remaining space.

When the stitching is complete, wash if necessary and press gently from the wrong side (see page 90). For finishing and mounting instructions, see page 92.

◆ **Above: Filled with symbols of fruitfulness and long life, this sampler also contains one of the sombre verses of which the Victorians were so fond.**

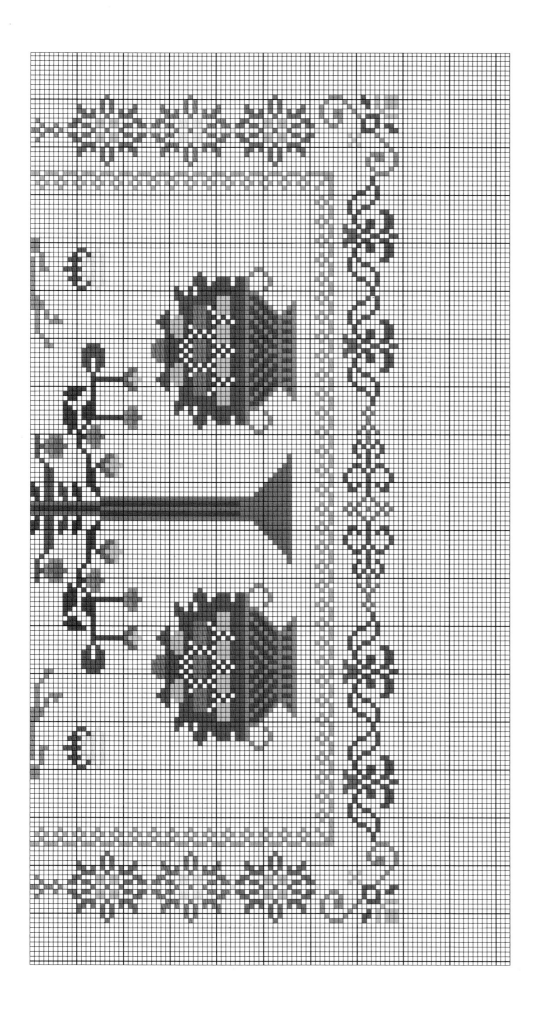

Book Cover

A corner design and cross from M.A. Tipper's sampler (the original at the Fitzwilliam Museum, Cambridge) is the inspiration for this design of a book cover, which would perhaps make a lovely confirmation or christening gift. I have included it as another example of how a study of the source material for the large samplers in this book can produce other useful motifs.

The Victorian sampler is typical of many worked at the time by children in schools, or more often in orphanages, and demonstrates the historical purpose of samplers which was as a functional way of teaching and developing needlecraft skills. The economical use of space together with the sheer number of patterns and stitches must have been the result of many hours of diligent work; practice in order to attain the necessary level of skill required for linen marking.

METHOD

Fold the rectangle in half with short sides together and crease lightly, then fold under 2 1/2 in (6.5 cm) at the righthand edge. Using a ruler,

◆ Right: A special design for a prized book.
Far right: A Bristol schoolchild's practice sampler, which is packed with several different styles of alphabets and numbers, a pious verse and a wide range of border patterns, all beautifully stitched.

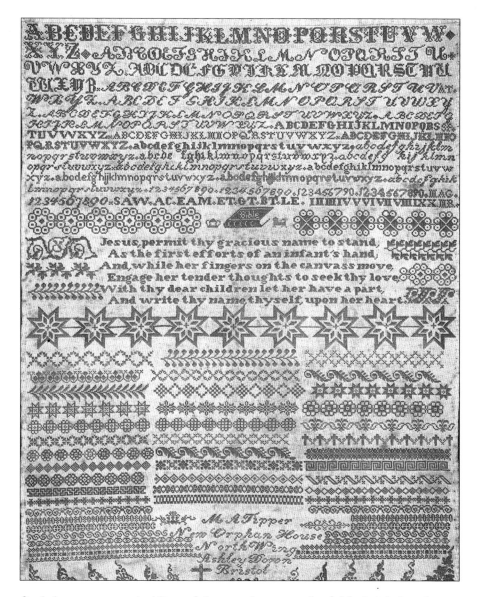

MATERIALS

1 piece of white Aida, 16 count, size to fit the book you wish to cover including 2 in (5 cm) flaps plus 1 in (2.5 cm) added to the width and to the depth

tapestry needle, size 26

1 piece of iron-on interfacing

braid or tassel

1 skein each of stranded cotton in the following shades:

		DMC	Anchor
▨	bronze	731	281
▨	pale brick red	760	9
▨	light pine green	581	280
▨	gold metallic		

Finished size of design: 2 5/8 x 2 5/8 in (6.5 x 6.5 cm)

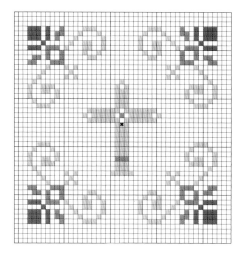

find the centre vertical line of the area between the folded righthand edge and the centre fold. Mark with tacking stitches. Fold under 1/2 in (1.5 cm) at the top and bottom, then mark the centre horizontal line in the same way. Begin stitching at the centre point following the starting stitch marked on the chart opposite.

Work in cross stitch using two strands of cotton over one thread intersection.

When the stitching is complete, remove any remaining tacking and press the fabric gently from the wrong side. Turn under a 1/2 in (1.5 cm) hem all round the fabric and slip stitch. Place the interfacing on the reverse of the fabric inside the hems and iron in position. Now turn under 2 in (5 cm) at both short ends to form the holding flaps and slip stitch the braid all along the top, bottom and fold side lines to follow the book cover edges. Stitch the folded flaps in place by slip stitching the fabric to the braid.

Cushion

The church scene for this project can be found on a Dutch sampler of 1844 now held in the Netherlands Open Air Museum in Arnhem. Little scenes of churches or houses in rural settings were often found in 19th century sampler work and one may wonder whether they are true representations of known or owned buildings or rather an idyllic version. The borders are further design motifs from the M. A. Tipper sampler used on the Symbolic Spot Sampler (see page 52).

METHOD

Fold the fabric in half lengthwise and crosswise to find the centre point. Crease lightly. Begin work at this point following the starting stitch marked on the chart on page 59.

Work in cross stitch using three strands of cotton over two thread intersections.

When the stitching is complete, press gently from the wrong side. If decorating with braid, place the embroidery and the backing fabric with right sides together. Pin and machine stitch or back stitch by hand round the sides, making a ½ in (1.5 cm) seam and leaving part of one side open. Trim across the corners, then turn right side out. Insert the cushion pad into the cover, then turn under the remaining raw edges and slip stitch the opening together.

Slip stitch the braid round the edges of the cushion over the seam and tuck the loose ends into the seam.

To include a frill, take the fabric for the frill, place the two short ends, right sides together, and stitch across the ends to form a circle. Press the seam open. Fold the circle in half lengthwise, wrong sides together and run a gathering stitch through both layers ½ in (1.5 cm) in from the raw edges. Gather and pin round the edges of the embroidered cushion side, right sides together and placing the raw edges of the frill to the raw edges of the cushion cover. Place the backing fabric on top, thus enclosing the frill and machine stitch or back stitch by hand as before. Turn right side out, releasing the frill, then continue as above, without the braid.

◆ Below: This charming spot sampler has provided motifs for our own sampler on page 52, as well as little devices for the greetings cards overleaf.

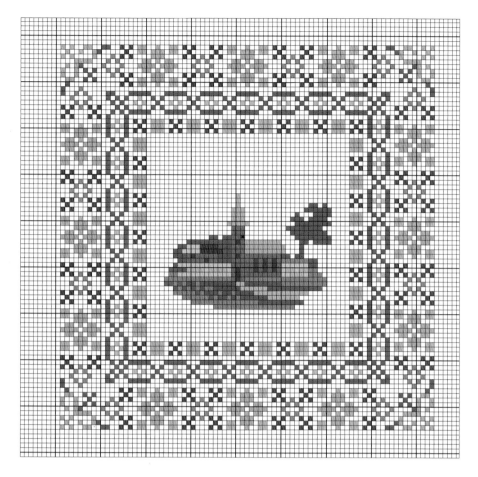

MATERIALS

2 pieces of ivory Lugana, 25 count or Linda, 27 count, 14 x 14 in (35 x 35 cm) or 1 piece of Linda or Lugana and a backing fabric of your choice

1 cushion pad, 12 in (31 cm) square

tapestry needle, size 24 or 26

1 ½ yds (1.5 m) braid or 2 ½ yds (2.5 m) of matching cotton, 4 in (10 cm) wide to make a frilled edge

1 skein each of stranded cotton in the following shades:

		DMC	Anchor
	dusty blue	334	977
	dark grey	413	401
	dark beige	436	363
	dark grey-green	501	878
	gold	783	307
	pale brick red	760	9
	wine red	816	44
	orange-brown	919	340
	antique green	3052	859

Finished size of design: 6 ½ x 6 ½ in (16.5 x 16.5 cm)

◆ A pastoral scene makes a restful image for a cushion cover.

Three Greeting Cards

Three more motifs taken from Sarah Robert's sampler (see page 58) are stitched here as decorations for a selection of greeting cards. The motifs could alternatively be incorporated into your own sampler designs.

The larger flower motif is of a tulip, which was a popular symbol denoting perfect love: for a Valentine's Day card? The tulip, which grows wild in Persia, is said to have sprung up on the spot where the tears of Ferhand fell after he had been rejected by Shirin, a young girl with whom he had fallen in love.

METHOD

Work as follows for all three designs.

Fold the fabric in half lengthwise and crosswise to find the centre point. Crease lightly. Begin work at this point following the starting stitch marked on the relevant chart.

Work in cross stitch using three strands of cotton over one thread intersection for the 14 count Aida and one strand over one intersection for the 22 count.

When the stitching is complete, press the fabric gently from the wrong side. Place the interfacing centrally on the reverse of the work and iron in position. Trim and mount in the cards following the instructions on page 92.

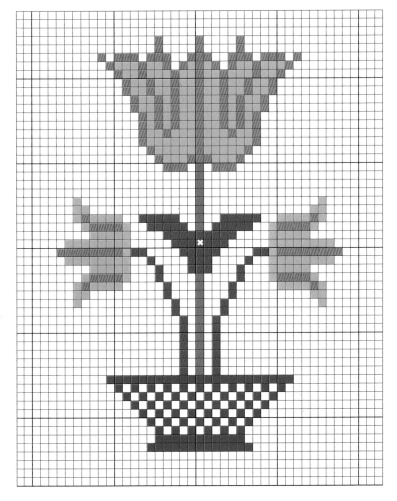

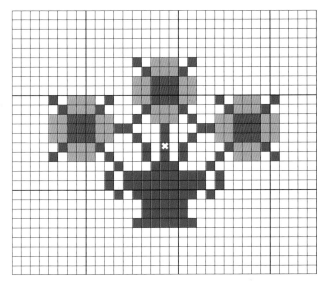

MATERIALS

1 piece of white Aida, 22 count, 5 x 5 in (12.5 x 12.4 cm), for the tulip design

2 pieces of white Aida, 14 count, 4 x 4 in (10 x 10 cm), for the yellow and pink flower designs

3 cards with the following apertures: 3¼ in (8 cm) circle; 2 in (5 cm) wide oval; 2¼ in (5.5 cm) wide arch (see page 93 for stockist)

tapestry needle, size 26

fabric adhesive

3 pieces of iron-on interfacing, same size as the pieces of Aida

1 skein each of stranded cotton in the following shades:

		DMC	Anchor
	new dark pink	3804	63
	new pink	3806	62
	new blue	3807	122
	new dark turquoise	3808	675
	new turquoise	3810	168
	new medium gold	3821	295
	new rust	3830	5975

Finished size of design, yellow flowers: 1⅓ x 1⅞ in (3.5 x 4.5 cm)

Finished size of design, tulip: 1⅔ x 2¼ in (4.5 x 6 cm)

Finished size of design, pink flowers: 1¼ x 1⅞ in (3 x 5 cm)

◆ **Left: Three useful patterns for greetings cards to suit a variety of occasions.**

William Morris Sampler

There is absolutely no doubt that William Morris' influence on the decorative and applied arts in the second half of the 19th century in England was monumental.

Graduating from Oxford and rejecting an original intention to enter the church, Morris instead joined the offices of an Oxford-based architect, G.E. Street. Then, through his friendship with Burne-Jones, a fellow graduate who had joined Dante Gabriel Rosetti with a view to becoming a painter, Morris, in his turn was encouraged by Rosetti to experiment with painting. The group, like most Victorians, was obsessed with all things medieval and Morris became increasingly involved in studying that age. However, unlike many of his contemporaries, he

◆ Right: A typical William Morris wallpaper pattern with symmetrical images intricately interlaced.
Far right: The colours and the central image of this sampler pay homage to William Morris' design style.

Materials

*1 piece of white Aida, 16 count,
18 ¾ x 16 ½ in (47 x 41.5 cm)*

tapestry needle(s), size 26

lightweight wadding for mounting (optional)

*1 skein each of stranded cotton in the
following shades:*

		DMC	Anchor
	medium green	320	215
	pale green	368	214
	very pale khaki	472	278
	v. pale petrol blue	747	928
	light petrol blue	518	168
	pale orange-brown	922	337
	light yellow	744	301
	fawn	676	891
	cream	746	386

2 skeins of stranded cotton in:

		DMC	Anchor
	buff	945	881
	very pale green	369	213
	pale petrol blue	519	167

*Finished size of design: 10 ¾ x 8 ½ in
(27.5 x 21.5 cm)*

found the ideals of the medieval way of life more attractive than the mere copying of Gothic style, which led him to reject the ornateness of these designs and to develop, as a reaction, his own inimitable style.

He formed various companies with other like-minded artists and designers through the subsequent years, the aim of which was the regeneration of all areas of the arts according to the medieval ideals of craftsmanship and the accompanying simple way of life. This ethos culminated in the formation of the Arts and Crafts Movement and the Century Guild of Artists which have left us with a legacy of superb designs encompassing glass, ceramics, metalwork, stained glass, textiles and furniture and have secured Morris' place in design history.

An aspect of design at which he particularly excelled was that of creating wallpaper patterns, one of which, called 'Lily and Pomegranate', is the influence for this project. It is one of his later designs (1886) and is a fine example of the mirror image structure typical of his work at this time. All Morris' wallpaper designs were hand-printed from woodblocks, a process which required enormous patience on the part of the crafts-man, as up to a dozen or more pearwood blocks might be required for a single pattern! The lily motif forms the central image of this sampler. The border is taken from a Berlin woolwork pattern of the late 19th century.

If you wish to personalize your work, enter a name or verse inside the rectangular box. If the name or verse is longer than the box allows, just omit the box and, using graph paper, chart out the words you wish to stitch based on the amount of fabric space available. Make sure that you leave at least two spaces between each line and three spaces between each word (see page 92). Alternatively, the sampler could be worked as a simple picture without text.

Method

As this is quite a detailed project that will take some time to complete, I strongly recommend that you hem or tack the raw edges of the fabric before starting to cross stitch, to prevent fraying (see page 90).

Fold the fabric in half lengthwise and crosswise, then mark these lines with tacking stitches. This will mark the centre point at which you start stitching on the fabric. Find the starting stitch marked on the chart on page 65 and begin work on the fabric with this stitch.

Use two strands of cotton, working over one thread intersection. Work the outlines in back stitch and the rest in cross stitch.

Work the flower motif first, leaving the back stitched outline until all the cross stitch areas have been completed. Next work the lower border, then the side borders, finishing with the top border. Now work the inter-nal rectangle above the flower motif and add your own personal details using the alphabet on pages 18 to 19. Finally, fill in the background.

When the stitching is complete, wash if necessary and press gently from the wrong side (see page 90). For finishing and mounting instructions, see page 92.

Picture Lily

Designed by C.R. Ashbee for the Guild of Handicraft, this silver inkwell, with enamelled panels is a beautiful adornment for any desk. Ashbee was at the forefront of the founding of this co-operative in 1888, which showed regularly at the Arts and Crafts Exhibitions.

The silver trade flourished during the Victorian period. Techniques such as the introduction of EPNS (electro-plated nickel silver) and the increased level of machine processing made silver cheaper to produce and therefore more affordable to many people. The cities of London, Birmingham and Sheffield produced most pieces ably assisted by the silversmiths of Dublin, Exeter, Chester and Edinburgh. Intricate styles and decoration embellished classical shapes, the artists taking their design themes from all periods of design history, with naturalistic subjects being the most popular.

◆ Below: A delightfully decorative silver and enamel inkwell of the late 19th century.

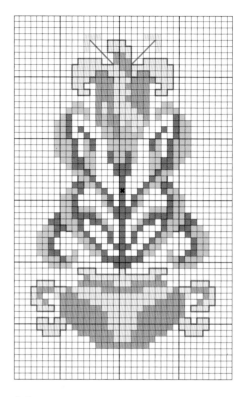

MATERIALS

1 piece of cream Aida, 18 count, 6 x 5 in (15 x 12.5 cm)

1 piece of iron-on interfacing, same size as Aida

lightweight wadding for mounting (optional)

1 picture frame, 3½ x 4½ in (9 x 11.5 cm)

tapestry needle, size 26

1 skein each of stranded cottons in the following shades:

		DMC	Anchor
	light gold	725	306
	gold	783	307
	light moss green	3347	266
	pale moss green	3348	264
backstitching			
	light moss green	*as above*	
	dark gold	781	309
	light blue	799	145

Finished size of design: 2⅞ x 1¾ in (7.5 x 4.5 cm)

◆ **Above: The potted lily motif makes a pretty picture.**

METHOD

Fold the fabric in half lengthwise and crosswise to find the centre point. Crease lightly. Start work at this point following the stitch marked on the chart above.

Work the cross stitch using two strands of cotton over one thread intersection. Work the back stitch using one strand of cotton over one thread intersection.

On completion rinse, press and iron on interfacing to the reverse of the design. Mount in the picture frame using wadding between the embroidery and backing board if liked.

Dressing Table Set

This design has been taken from a stained glass window depicting St Ferdinand which is to be found in the royal chapel at Dreux in France. It was made by the Sèvres factory in 1846 and makes use of enamelling for the figure. The borders and canopies were designed by Viollet-le-Duc and the cartoon for the saint by Ingrès. I have worked it in pastel colours but the thread shades could easily be changed to complement your own bedroom colour scheme.

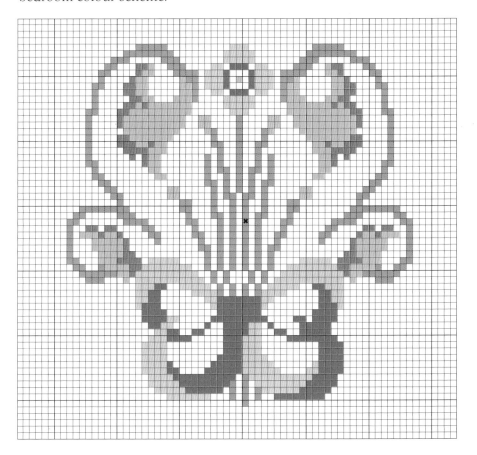

METHOD

Work as follows for both pieces.

Fold the fabric in half lengthwise and crosswise to find the centre point. Crease lightly. Begin work at this point following the starting stitch marked on the chart above.

Work in cross stitch using two strands of cotton over one thread intersection.

When the stitching is complete, press the fabric gently from the wrong side. Place the interfacing centrally on the reverse of the work and iron in position. Trim and place the fabric centrally in the mount following the manufacturer's instructions.

MATERIALS

Dressing Table Set

1 piece of white Aida, 18 count, 7 x 7 in (18 x 18 cm), for the mirror

1 piece of white Aida, 18 count, 5 x 6 in (12.5 x 15 cm), for the hairbrush

tapestry needle, size 26

2 pieces of iron-on interfacing, same size as the pieces of Aida

1 dressing table set (see page 93 for stockist)

1 skein each of stranded cotton in the following shades:

		DMC	Anchor
	very pale pink	605	50
	light maroon	3687	68
	fawn	676	891
	light yellow	744	300
	light blue	799	145
	very pale blue	800	144
	pea green	989	242

Finished size of design: 3 x 3 in (7.5 x 7.5 cm)

MATERIALS

Pincushion

2 pieces cream Aida, 14 count, 5 x 5 in (12.5 x 12.5 cm)

1 tapestry needle, size 24

polyester filling

cream sewing thread and sewing needle

braid in your choice of colour, 26 in (66 cm) long, and/or corner tassels

1 skein each of stranded cottons in the following shades:

		DMC	Anchor
	medium blue-green	562	210
	pale sea blue	827	9159
	pale green-gold	834	874
	light maroon	3687	68
	pale dusty pink	3689	49

Finished size of design: 2 3/4 x 2 3/4 in (7 x 7 cm)

◆ **Far left: A scrolling floral design from a 19th century French stained glass window has inspired the motif for the mirror and hairbrush set (above).**

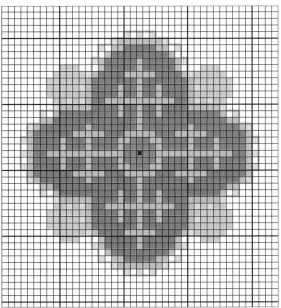

Pincushion

The centre quatrefoil of a Gothic-styled gold and champlevé enamel headband, designed by A.W.N. Pugin is the inspiration for this small project. Worked singly here as a pincushion, it could also be used as the corner motifs on a sampler or repeated in a line as a border for linen. Alternatively it could be stitched in metallic threads to decorate an evening bag.

◆ Below: The quatrefoil is perhaps the most typical shape of the Victorian Gothic style. Pugin, the architect and interior designer, made great use of it, even on jewellery (right). We have featured it prominently on this little pincushion.
Far right: The shape of the bookmark makes a perfect display area for this pretty floral design.

METHOD

Fold one of the pieces of Aida in half lengthwise and crosswise to find the centre point. Crease lightly. Start work on the fabric at this point following the stitch marked on the chart on page 69.

Use two strands of cotton worked over one thread intersection for the cross stitch and one strand of cotton for the back stitch.

When the stitching is complete, press the fabric gently from the wrong side. Place the two pieces of Aida right sides together and machine stitch or back stitch by hand around three sides of the square, leaving a ¼ in (6 mm) seam allowance. Trim the corners, then turn right side out. Fill the cushion with the stuffing to the desired density, then turn under the seam allowance on the open side and slip stitch to close.

Stitch the braid around all four edges of the cushion, looping it at the corners if you wish and tucking the ends into the seam allowance. Alternatively you could attach tassels at the corners.

Bookmark

A letter embosser in my own collection of Victoriana provides the inspiration for this project. How much prettier it is than its modern day equivalents! This design could easily be adapted and the flower colours altered to your own choice of shades, using the motif on door plates or stationery or as a repeat pattern on a cushion cover.

METHOD

Fold the bookmark in half lengthwise and crosswise to find the centre point. Crease lightly. Start work at this point following the stitch marked on the chart opposite.

Work the cross stitch using two strands of cotton over one thread intersection. Work the back stitch using one strand of cotton over one thread intersection.

When the stitching is complete, wash if necessary and press gently from the wrong side (see page 90).

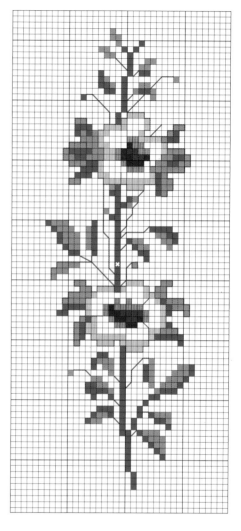

MATERIALS

1 lacy bookmark (see page 93 for stockist)
tapestry needle, size 26
1 skein each of stranded cotton in the following shades:

		DMC	Anchor
	dark grey	413	401
	brown	975	370
	dark pea green	986	246
	pea green	989	242
	pale dusty rose	3354	74
	dusty rose	3731	38

backstitching

	dark pea green	as above
	dusty rose	as above

Finished size of design: 4 1/4 x 1 1/2 in (11 x 4 cm)

MATERIALS

design A

1 piece of white Aida, 18 count, see method for size

tapestry needle, size 26

stiff white card

fabric adhesive

1 piece of iron-on interfacing, same size as Aida

braid (optional)

1 skein each of stranded cotton in the following shades:

		DMC	Anchor
▉	blue	798	131
▨	pale blue	809	130
▨	pale green-gold	834	874

Finished size of design (single motif): 4⅓ x 1 in (11 x 2.5 cm)

design B

1 piece of cream Aida, 16 count, see method for size

tapestry needle, size 26

stiff white card

fabric adhesive

1 piece of iron-on interfacing, same size as Aida

1 skein each of stranded cotton in the following shades:

		DMC	Anchor
▨	gold	676	891
▉	new turquoise	3810	168

Finished size of design (single motif): 7 x 9¼ in (17.5 x 23 cm)

Photograph Borders

These two designs were inspired by an old postcard issued by the government of Victoria, Australia in 1898. Many antique fairs have stands selling old postcards, which can be purchased at very reasonable prices and can prove a wonderful source of design inspiration quite apart from their intrinsic fascination. These designs can be adapted in size to fit the photograph and frame you wish to use.

The instructions describe how to cover a window mount for the photograph but you could simply fix the picture in the middle of the embroidered fabric as shown in one of the frames below.

METHOD

To estimate the amount of fabric required, measure the frame in which you wish to place the photograph and border, then add on 1 in (2.5 cm) all round e.g. for a frame measuring 6 x 8 in (15 x 20 cm), you will need a piece of fabric 8 x 10 in (20 x 25 cm). Next cut a piece of stiff white card to the frame size. Place the photograph you wish to mount centrally on the card and mark around the perimeter in pencil onto the card. Now cut out the square or rectangle ½ in (1 cm) smaller than the marked dimensions to cover any border round the photograph.

Fold the fabric in half lengthwise and crosswise to find the centre

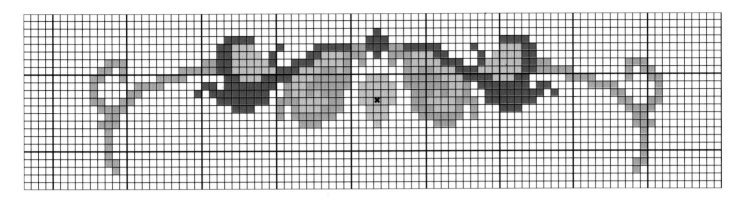

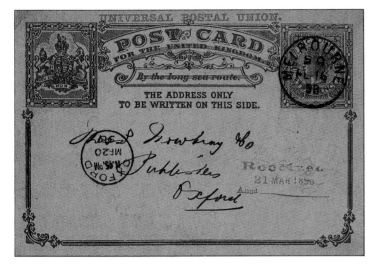

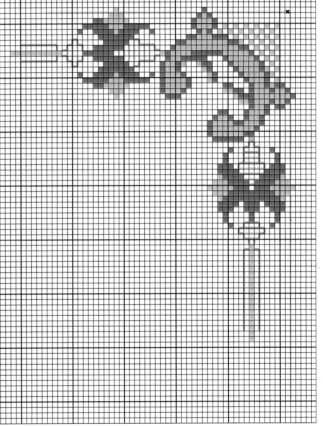

point. Crease lightly. Place the cut-out onto your fabric, then pin the place at the centre of the top where you wish to position the border pattern. Match this with the centre point on the chart for design A and commence stitching at this point. For design B, measure 1 in (2.5 cm) down from the top right corner of the fabric and 1 in (2.5 cm) in from the righthand side, and begin stitching at this point following the point marked on the chart on the right.

Work in cross stitch and back stitch using two strands of cotton over one thread intersection. Work the complete corner motif. Repeat for the opposite corner, then join them with the straight border lines and finally work the back stitched frame all round the outside.

On completion rinse if necessary, press gently and back with interfacing. Place the cut-out card centrally under the worked fabric and pin round the window opening, then gently, from the centre of the fabric, cut four diagonal lines to within ¼ in (6 mm) of the corners. Trim the points of the triangles formed and glue the fabric overlaps to the wrong side of the cut-out. Now fix the photograph behind the worked piece and place in the frame of your choice. Slip stitch braid round the opening if liked.

Top: design A
Above: design B

◆ **Left: Decorative borders from this early postcard have inspired the stitched borders which frame two old Victorian photographs (far left).**

Desk Pen Set

The stained glass window inspiring this project is a fine example of the Victorians' love of historicism demonstrated by their reworking of design principles and styles from bygone ages. It is the work of the French firm of A.N. Didron. The panel may be viewed at Feltwell, Norfolk. It has a repeat design as the background pattern, which has been reinterpreted to form the decoration for a desk pen set. The motif could be worked singly for gift tags or cards, or as a central motif on napkins with complementary coasters.

METHOD

Fold the fabric in half lengthwise and crosswise to find the centre point. Crease lightly. Begin work at this point following the starting stitch marked on the chart on page 77.

Work in cross stitch using one strand of cotton over one thread intersection. When the stitching is complete, press the fabric gently from the wrong side. Place the interfacing centrally on the reverse of the work and iron in position. Trim and place the fabric centrally in the mount following the manufacturer's instructions.

MATERIALS

1 piece of cream Aida, 22 count, 5 x 5 in (12.5 x 12.5 cm)

1 desk pen set (see page 93 for stockist)

1 piece of iron-on interfacing, same size as Aida

tapestry needle, size 26

1 skein each of stranded cotton in the following shades:

		DMC	Anchor
	pale navy	312	979
	dark maroon	814	45
	dark green-gold	832	907
	very dark khaki	937	268

Finished size of design: 2 ¾ x 2 ¾ in (7 x 7 cm)

◆ Right: Many stained glass windows have interesting background patterns, such as this one which has inspired the motif for the desk pen set (above).

Collector's Cabinet

A motif from a Silesian sampler of 1833 stitched by Marie Brehm is used here as decoration for a collector's cabinet. The motif could equally well be worked onto a pot lid or mounted into a card as a gift for a gardening enthusiast.

MATERIALS

1 piece of white Aida, 18 count, 5 x 5 in (12.5 x 12.5 cm)

1 collector's cabinet (see page 93 for stockist)

1 piece of iron-on interfacing, same size as Aida

tapestry needle, size 26

1 skein each of stranded cotton in the following shades:

		DMC	Anchor
	blue	798	131
	pale blue	809	130
	moss green	3346	267
	pale moss green	3348	264
	dusky pink	3688	66
	new pale gold	3822	305
	light maroon	3687	68

Finished size of design: 3 ⅛ x 2 ¾ in (8 x 7 cm)

METHOD

Fold the fabric in half lengthwise and crosswise to find the centre point. Crease lightly. Begin work at this point following the starting stitch marked on the chart on page 77.

Work in cross stitch using two strands of cotton over one thread intersection.

When the stitching is complete, press the fabric gently from the wrong side. Place the interfacing centrally on the reverse of the work and iron in position. Trim carefully to fit the backing card, then assemble according to the manufacturer's instructions.

◆ Above: A detail from a German sampler shown in full on page 13. Left: Given the Victorians' passion for collecting, this motif from a 19th century sampler makes a particularly suitable decoration for the display cabinet.

MATERIALS

For a pair of tie-backs:

2 pieces of white Aida, 11 count, each 27 x 15 in (68 x 38 cm)

tapestry needle(s), 24

2 pieces of backing fabric, same size as Aida

2 pieces of heavy duty stiffening, each 25 x 6 ½ in (63.5 x 16.5 cm)

4 ring hooks and wall attachments of your own choice

2 yds (2 m) braid in complementary colour

1 skein each of stranded cotton in the following shades:

		DMC	Anchor
	dark rose pink	309	42
	medium rose pink	335	41
	v. dark rose pink	326	59
	pale rose pink	3326	36
	rose pink	899	40
	dark dusty blue	322	978
	pale dusty blue	3325	129
	light dusty blue	3755	140
	dark peach	351	10
	peach	352	9
	pale peach	353	6
	yellow	743	305
	blue	798	131
	pale blue	809	130
	v. dark moss green	895	269
	dark moss green	3345	268
	light moss green	3347	266
	pale moss green	3348	264
	pale orange-brown	922	337

2 skeins of stranded cotton in:

	moss green	3346	267

Finished size of design: 4 ¼ x 14 ¼ in (11 x 36 cm)

◆ **Right: A typical Berlin woolwork design: its rich colours made more vibrant by the dark background.**

Tie-backs

Part of a beautiful piece of Berlin woolwork, held at St Fagan's Museum forms the basis for this embroidery. The great swags and drapes that framed the windows of a Victorian home often had elaborate tie-backs. A return to popularity of the tie-back today, inspires this project.

METHOD

To work the righthand tie-back, fold the fabric in half crosswise with long edges together, then measure 2 in (5 cm) along this crease from the short right side edge. Begin work at this point following the top two starting stitches marked on the chart on page 77.

For the lefthand tie-back, measure the same distance along the crease but this time from the lefthand short edge. Begin work at this point following the bottom two starting stitches on the chart. Work in cross stitch using three strands of cotton over one thread intersection.

When the stitching is complete, wash if necessary and press gently from the wrong side (see page 90). Still working on the wrong side of the embroidery, lightly mark the tie-back shape in pencil, leaving approximately ½ in (1.5 cm) of unworked fabric at top and bottom of the deepest part of the design and roughly 2 in (5 cm) at each end. The shape is basically a rectangle with rounded ends. Place the stitched piece on top of the backing fabric with right sides together. Pin and machine stitch or backstitch by hand round the marked shape, leaving half of one long side open. Trim the seam allowance to ¼ in (6 mm). Turn right side out, press and turn under the raw edges of the opening. Cut the stiffening to the same shape as the tie-back and place inside the tie-back. Slip stitch both sides of the opening together, leaving a small gap to take the ends of the braid and keeping the fabric taut over the stiffening. Attach the braid round the edge, tucking the ends into the gap in the seam. Finally, stitch the rings to the back of the tie-back, one in the centre of each end.

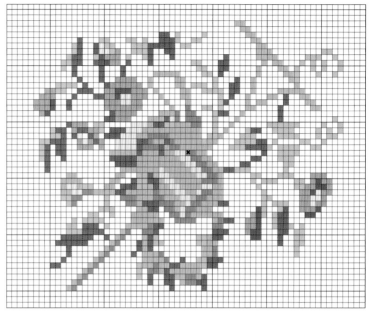

Top: Collector's Cabinet
Left: Tie-backs
Above: Desk Pen Set

77

Towel

This flowing design comes from another section of the Berlin woolwork panel shown with the previous project. It has been worked as a towel decoration but could look equally effective as a border for a commemorative sampler.

METHOD

Work as follows for either type of towel.

Fold the towel in half lengthwise to find the centre vertical line and mark with pins on the flatweave bands, then tack. Next fold each band in half crosswise and mark with a pin, then with tacking thread, the point at which this fold crosses the vertical line. This gives the central point of each band.

For the purchased towel, attach the waste canvas (see page 89) and use the darning needle. For the kitchen towel, use the tapestry needle.

For both towels, begin stitching at the central point, following the marked stitch on the chart below.

Work in cross stitch using three strands of cotton worked over one thread intersection. If liked, you could continue to work motifs on either side of the first, leaving one square between each and repeating the pattern as many times as you wish. Starting in the centre will ensure that the pattern will be evenly balanced on the band.

Once the stitching over the waste canvas is complete, gently withdraw the canvas threads using tweezers.

MATERIALS

1 purchased towel with a flatweave band at each end in your own choice of size and colour or 18 count kitchen towel (see page 93 for stockist)

waste fabric, 14 count, length to match the width of your towel or the width of the number of repeats you wish to sew (purchased towel only)

tapestry needle, size 24 (kitchen towel only)

sharp-pointed darning needle (purchased towel only)

1 skein each of stranded cotton in the following shades:

		DMC	Anchor
	dark peach	351	10
	v. dark grey-green	500	879
	light bright green	911	230
	pale bright green	913	204
	pale peach	353	6

Finished size of design (single motif): 1½ x 4½ in (4 x 12 cm)

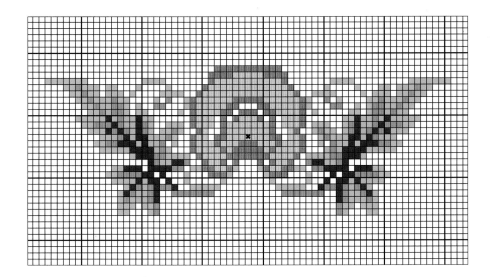

◆ **Far left: The towel and the tie-back both owe their realistic designs to an original Berlin woolwork piece.**

MATERIALS

1 piece of 14 count white Aida, 27 x 9 in (68.5 x 23 cm)

1 circular piece of 14 count white Aida, 7¾ in (19.5 cm) in diameter

1 piece of wadding, 25 x 9 in (63.5 x 23 cm)

1 circular piece of wadding, 7¾ in (19.5 cm) in diameter

1 piece of lining, 27 x 9 in (68.5 x 23 cm)

1 circular piece of lining, 7¾ in (19.5 cm) in diameter

tapestry needle, size 24

1 piece of cord, 1 yd (1 m) long

½ in (15 mm) seam binding to match lining, 25 in (63.5 cm) long

white sewing cotton

1 skein each of stranded cotton in the following shades:

		DMC	Anchor
	new turquoise	3810	168
	new pale gold	3822	305
	new rust	3830	5975

Finished size of design (single motif): 5 x 6 in (12.5 x 15 cm)

Workbag

This design is based upon a pair of scissors elaborately engraved with the arms of the Cavendish family, made by G. Wilkinson and displayed at the Great Exhibition of 1851. Part of the design would make an interesting border pattern, especially if a little motif were entered within the circles. It is stitched here in repeat form to decorate a workbag.

METHOD

Measure 3 in (7.5 cm) down from the top right corner of the fabric and 3 in (7.5 cm) in from the righthand side Begin stitching at this point following the point marked on the chart on page 81. Work in cross stitch and back stitch using two strands of cotton over one thread intersection. Repeat the motif four times along the fabric, leaving 1 in (2.5 cm)

◆ **Far right: One of the many pieces on show at the Great Exhibition in 1851. Right: A pretty workbag for display and for essential storage.**

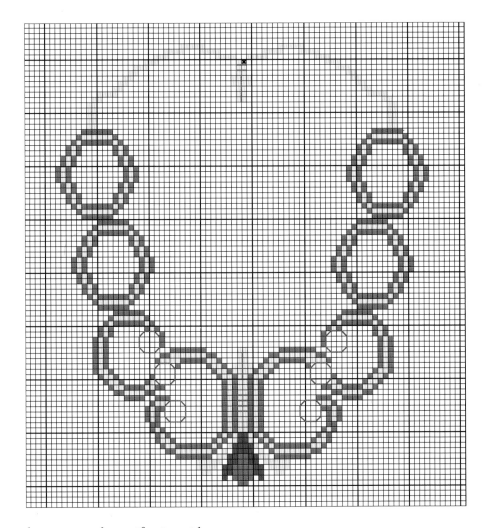

between each motif at its widest part.

When the stitching is complete, press lightly from the wrong side, then place the two short sides of the fabric together with the embroidery on the inside. Stitch, taking a 1¼ in (3 cm) seam. Trim, press open and neaten the edges. Do the same with the lining.

Place the wadding round the wrong side of the Aida and tack the overlap. Tack round the top edge. Place the lining tube inside the Aida, right sides together and stitch round the top edge, taking a ¼ in (6 mm) seam. Fold the lining to the outside of the tube and press the seam.

Pin the seam binding to the lining 1½ in (4 cm) down from the top of the tube, turning under the raw edges on either side of the seam. Stitch through all three layers along the top and bottom of the binding.

Next sandwich the wadding circle between the Aida and lining circle and tack together round the outside. Pin to the base of the tube, right sides together. Stitch, taking a ½ in (6 mm) seam. Remove tacking. Trim the seam and oversew to neaten.

Turn right side out, make an opening in the straight seam at the level of the binding and thread the cord through the sleeve made by the binding. Knot the ends to secure.

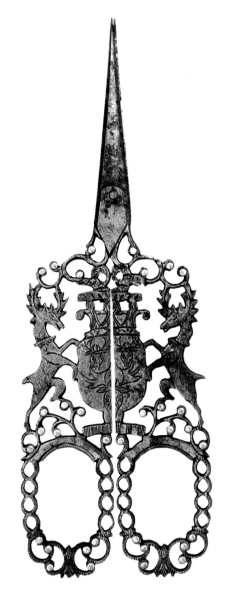

Flower Basket Picture

The fascination with early colour printing meant that postcard greetings were extremely popular in the Victorian era and were printed in large numbers. They made a pleasant and effective way of sending a short message. The motif inspired by this French thank you card has been worked as picture but on a smaller count fabric could form a lovely Mother's Day card.

◆ Right: This French greetings card from the 1900s is typical of the mass-printed designs of the period. It has inspired the little picture opposite.

MATERIALS

1 piece of white Aida, 16 count, 7½ x 6 in (19 x 15 cm)

tapestry needle, size 26

1 piece of iron-on interfacing, same size as Aida

lightweight wadding for mounting (optional)

picture frame, with 3¼ x 4¾ in (8.5 x 12 cm) window mount

1 skein each of stranded cotton in the following shades:

		DMC	Anchor
	pink	603	62
	very pale pink	605	50
	dark grey	413	401
	pale blue-green	564	206
	pea green	989	242
	fawn	676	891
	coffee	3045	888
	pale gold	726	295
	gold	783	307

Finished size of design: 3¼ x 2 in (8 x 5 cm)

METHOD

To make the picture, fold the fabric in half lengthwise and crosswise. Crease lightly to mark the centre point at which you start stitching on the fabric. Find the centre starting stitch marked on the chart on page 82 and begin work on the fabric with this stitch, using two strands of cotton over one thread intersection. Work in cross stitch for the main design and back stitch for the details.

When the stitching is complete, rinse if necessary and press the fabric gently from the wrong side.

Trim and mount in the picture frame, using wadding in between the embroidery and the backing board if you so wish.

Chart-only samplers

The following pages feature two pieces of original source material linked to fully charted adaptations for you to incorporate into your own sampler designs. The designs are an interesting contrast: one is the work of a prominent designer for commercial reproduction, the other displays the efforts of a schoolgirl practising her embroidery skills and perhaps learning her alphabet at the same time. Both pieces can be stitched by following the charts exactly and will make stunning samplers in their own right. Alternatively, they can be adapted to your own requirements or split up and used as a motif library.

Details on how to estimate the size of fabric required are given on page 92.

PAGES 85 TO 86

VICTORIAN ALPHABET SAMPLER

This simple sampler is worked entirely in cross stitch on a fine white linen. It is all accurately stitched with each row of letters placed in exactly the same position on succeeding lines but although the alphabet is repeated four times, there are different borders to separate each line.

The charted version gives you the opportunity of producing a miniature version by working just one upper case and one lower case alphabet on a fine count of fabric. It has been charted in bright colours for a livelier effect.

Alternatively, the letters can be used to personalize other commemorative sampler work and the simple borders will make useful frames for the text.

PAGES 87 TO 88

AUTUMN FLOWERS SAMPLER

This is another of William Morris' wallpaper designs. His first set of designs was produced commercially in 1864. This pattern, called 'Autumn Flowers', is from a later period. It was produced in 1880 and it is a prime example of what Morris himself described as 'the conventionalising of nature'. He took natural forms and rearranged them into symmetrical shapes while still retaining recognisable flowers and leaves. The designs cleverly cover the whole surface and are full of movement.

The charted design could be worked on a dark background to reflect the colouring of the original. It would work well as a picture but you could also take up Morris' theme and use separate elements in repeated blocks to produce your own symmetrical designs either for a centrepiece or for a border.

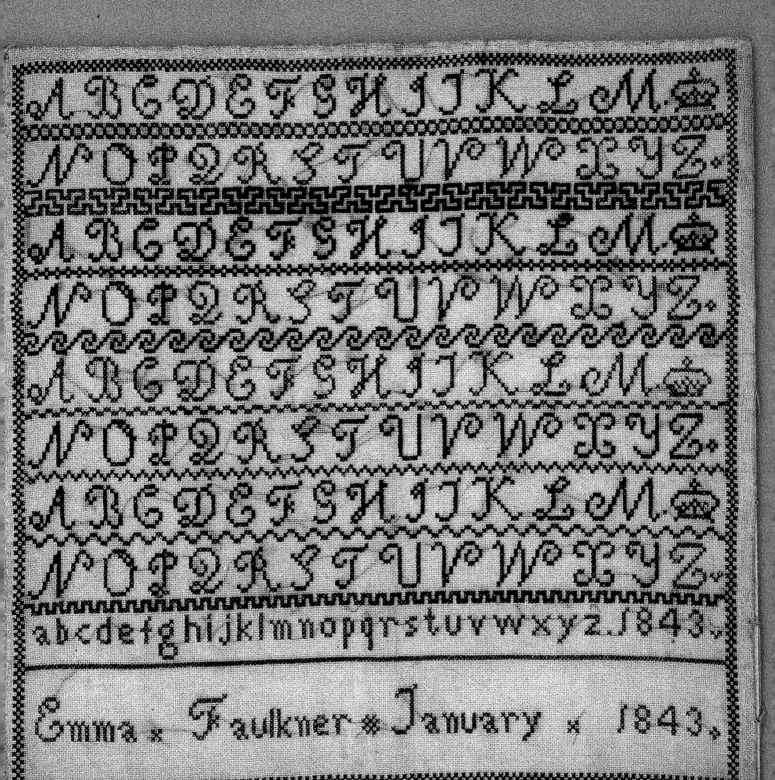

Emma × Faulkner × January × 1843.

Practical Details

FABRICS

Cross stitch is mostly worked on evenweave fabrics - those which have a well-defined, equal warp (vertical) and weft (horizontal) thread, woven in such a way that there are the same number of warp as of weft threads in any square of fabric. Evenweave fabric comes in a variety of types and sizes, which are graded according to the number of threads or holes per inch with the highest number denoting the finest weave and consequently producing the finest stitch. This grading of fabric is referred to as the 'count' of the fabric, so that 18 count fabric will have 18 holes and threads to the inch (2.5 centimetres). Grades range from 10 count through to 26. If a novice, I suggest you start with projects on a lower count (14, for example) and when you are conversant with the basic skill move to the finer or higher counts.

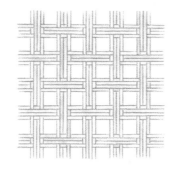

Aida is a widely available type of evenweave fabric and many of the projects in this book are worked on it in various counts. It is woven with groups of warp and weft threads bulked together and woven as one unit, which leaves clearly defined holes between and makes it easy to see where to place the stitches.

Hardanger, a type of evenweave in which pairs of threads are woven together, is also available and the same principles apply.

Lugana is another type of evenweave. A 25 count is available in a variety of shades and is a lovely fabric for bellpulls and wall hangings, as it is softer than Aida but weightier, so that it hangs well. It also has the advantage that, like linens, it can be worked over one or two threads.

Also featured in this book are products made from 'Sal-Em' fabric, an American-produced fabric, cut to the shape of napkins or traycloths with frayed edges and a pre-stitched line around the edges to prevent further fraying. It can be used either for fine stitches worked over one thread to form 26 count or over two threads to form 13 count. If unavailable, a 26 count linen could be used. You could, then, either hem or fray the edges yourself.

Linen is also suitable. This is a plain-weave, i.e. a fabric in which a single weft is woven alternately over and under a single warp, but is still suitable for cross-stitch work as the weaving of the warp and weft threads is equally spaced throughout the fabric.

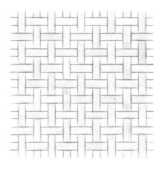

Special silk fabric is also used, this has a very high count and needs to be stretched into a frame, to make it manageable for stitching. It is available in pre-stretched form (see page 93) and is supplied with a fine needle. Make sure you are working in a good, bright light when stitching silk, as it is very fine work.

All the fabrics come in a variety of shades and colours. I have used mostly cream and white in this series, but do try experimenting with other shades. Maybe your specialist needlecraft store has a few remnant pieces you could try at not too high a cost for experimentation.

Waste canvas

Other fabrics can be used if your eye and patience are good, but do not attempt to use these until you have mastered the craft.

Waste canvas, available from specialist stores can help with the stitching of non-defined fabric, that is fabric which does not have an obvious grid of threads to work over, such as towelling or velvet. Waste canvas provides a temporary grid, which can be removed after it has been stitched over.

Pin or tack a piece of waste canvas 1 in (2.5 cm) larger all round than the design to be stitched onto the fabric you wish to embroider. Work your stitches over it but be careful not to pull up the stitches too tightly. Once the stitching is

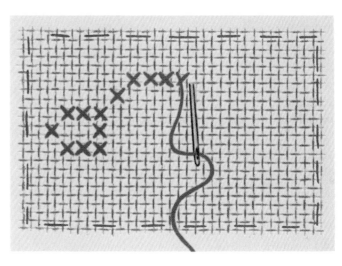

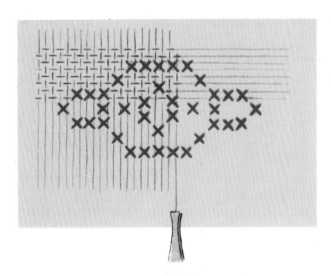

completed, draw out the threads of the waste canvas one by one with tweezers. They should release quite easily as long as your tension has not been too severe!

Care of fabric

All the evenweaves and linen launder beautifully and the stranded cottons used throughout the books are colourfast. If you are in any doubt about whether your threads are colourfast, do a test wash using a little of all the colours on a small piece first. When you have completed your project, if you feel it has become slightly grubby from handling, just wash gently in warm, soapy water, then rinse, to revitalise it. You will also be able to re-stiffen the evenweave Aida by doing this, which will make it easier to mount, as it does tend to soften while being worked. Roll up the embroidery in a dry towel to take out excess moisture, then leave the work on a flat surface to dry naturally. When dry, gently press the embroidery from the wrong side on a dry towel base with a medium-hot steam iron. The fabric can also be given a gentle press in this way during the stitching of a large project, if you feel it has become too limp.

THREADS

Every shade imaginable can be purchased! Half the fun is deciding which to use. Metallic threads are also popular and can add quite a sparkle to your work but the mainstay thread for cross stitch is stranded cotton. It is so-called because each thread is made up of six strands, which are separated to work with, the number of strands altering dependent on the count of the fabric.

As a rough guide on 10 to 14 count use three strands (unless the design is so dense you prefer to use two strands on 14); on 16 to 22 use two strands and on higher counts, one strand.

Other threads, such as crochet cotton, Danish flower threads, coton à broder and stranded silk are also suitable for cross stitch, though the thicker single strand threads should only be used on low counts of fabric.

Use of threads

As suggested, use different numbers of strands for different counts of fabric but universally do not thread your needle with more than a 14 in (35 cm) length at any time. A longer thread will eventually fray in the needle as it is drawn repeatedly through the fabric and leave a feathery thread on the stitching; it may, indeed, even fray out and break.

NEEDLES

Always use blunt-ended tapestry needles. The general rule regarding size is that the eye of the needle should be able to pass through the fabric without distorting the weave and leaving a larger hole. Size 24 is perfect for counts up to 14 and size 26 is fine for other higher counts; on silk use an even finer needle - size 28 or higher - as these are often up to 48 count!

FRAMES

Hoop frames are often used to prevent distortion of the fabric caused by an over-tight tension. Try a small one if you wish, your needlecraft shop will advise you and let you handle the various sizes to see which is comfortable for you. Personally, I only use one when working with floppy fabrics to help keep my tension even. I find generally I like to be able to manoeuvre the fabric in my hands without the constraint of the hoop, the natural stiffness of some fabrics being enough to keep tension balanced. So, whether or not to use a frame is very much your choice.

SETTING TO WORK

Before starting fix a short piece of each thread to a strip of card and number it. This will help you identify the shade, invaluable if you find yourself working in a poor light (which should be avoided) or artificial light when tones, particularly of blues, greens and pinks can subtly alter.

With larger projects it is best (time consuming, I know) to protect the edges of the fabric to prevent fraying, which linen, in particular, is prone to do. To do this, either turn under a small hem all round and tack down or bind the edges with masking tape. This is generally unnecessary with small projects.

The starting point on a stitching chart is generally indicated, as is the case for all the projects in these books. For small designs this is usually in the centre, so that it is helpful to be able to find the centre of your fabric quickly. To do this fold the fabric in half lengthwise and crosswise and crease lightly. For larger projects you may find it useful to tack through the centre vertical and horizontal lines created by folding the fabric, so that these provide permanent reference points when stitching the design. On smaller projects just the creased cross should be enough to get you started. Some patterns give the start stitch in one corner or in the middle of one edge of the pattern, so you will not need to do the above tacking or creasing, just follow the instructions as to the start point.

Thread your needle with the directed number of strands. Do not knot the end as this creates lumps which make an uneven surface on the embroidery and knots can unravel. To commence the first stitch, pull the thread through from the reverse side leaving a tail of about 2 inches (5 cm).

◆ **Single cross stitch**

 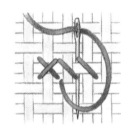

◆ **Cross stitch row**

Hold this tail under the fabric as you work the next stitch. After a few stitches you can either darn the tail in at the back or catch it under with the subsequent stitches. Fasten off by drawing the thread, on the reverse side, through the back of some stitches.

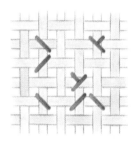

◆ **Half cross stitch**

All the projects in this book use simple cross stitch for most of the design, half cross stitch for some of the shaping and back stitch for outlining. Use the simple half cross stitch for shaping on the edge of a motif and the three quarters version when required in the middle of a design.

If you are a novice, follow the diagrams on a spare piece of fabric to practise.

It is important that the top half of the stitches should all slant in the same direction, otherwise the finished work will look uneven.

All the patterns are worked from colour charts. One square on the chart represents one stitch worked over one or two thread inter-sections on the fabric as directed in the individual instructions. Half squares on the chart denote half cross

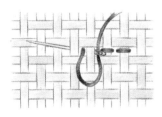

◆ **Backstitch**

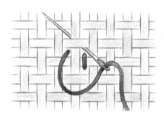

◆ **Angled backstitch**

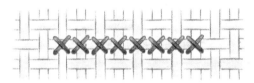

◆ **Over one thread intersection**

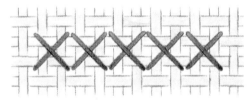

◆ **Over two thread intersections**

stitches, the direction of the diagonal indicating the direc-tion of the stitch. If stitches of one shade are scattered close by each other but not immediately abutting each other, it is acceptable to thread the strands through the backs of some of the other stitches to the next point of stitching, but do this only where there is close proximity of stitch, otherwise the overall tension will become distorted.

Using more than one needle

It is useful, when working a design where groups of stitches in the same shade are close to each other, to use more than one needle. When you have stitched the first group, take the needle through to the reverse of the fabric and secure it loosely in a position where it will not interfere with the next stitches you will work. Using the second needle, work the second shade and fasten the needle at the back of the work, as before. Now remove the first needle and thread it through the back of the stitches just worked, so that it is in the right position to work the second group of stitches in the first shade. This can only be done where groups of stitches in the same shade are separated by just three or four squares. If you carry thread over a larger distance, you may produce an uneven tension and on a low count of fabric the lines of thread may show through to the front.

It is also helpful to have several needles threaded with different shades at the start of a complicated project. This saves time once you are stitching.

Estimating fabric size

The finished size of the stitching area is given with each project, so that if you wish to adapt the design you can work out how the dimensions will change.

If you wish to work one of the projects in this book on a different count of fabric from that recommended, you will need to calculate how much fabric to allow, which is very simple. Count the number of squares on the design chart a) down one vertical edge and b) across one horizontal edge. Divide each of these figures by the count of the fabric you wish to use, e.g. by 14 or 16. This will give you the finished design size in inches. Multiply by 2.54 if you wish to have the size in centimetres.

If the work is to be mounted in a frame, add 6 in (15 cm) to each dimension for the fabric size. This allows a good 3 in (7.5 cm) for the framer to use and a 1 in (2.5 cm) hem allowance (to prevent fraying while working).

For fabric size on smaller projects, add 3 in (7.5 cm) to the dimensions of the design, and to fit a particular mount, measure its width and depth, then add on 3 in (7.5 cm).

Letter spacing

This is best worked out on graph paper first, to give a good visual image of how the letters will look. Map out the letters in each horizontal row in pencil on the graph paper, leaving one stitch square between each letter and three between each word. Note that letters which have sloping sides, such as A, W, V, may look better more closely grouped, i.e. without the unstitched square in between.

Now count up the number of horizontal squares in the row and divide by two to find the central point. Where the letters are to be placed centrally on the design, this point will correspond to the centre vertical line of the design. Begin stitching at this point.

For designs where the text is positioned off-centre, refer to the appropriate chart for the starting point. Do map out the letters on graph paper first, though, as you may need to adjust the placing slightly.

FINISHING OFF AND MOUNTING

Tidy your work as you stitch, fastening each thread off by darning it into the back other stitches. Snip off any loose ends.

If the piece needs to be cleaned or freshened up, follow the instructions for washing and pressing given above.

Mounting into card-based mounts, e.g. calendars, greeting cards

Trim the finished piece of work to a slightly smaller size than the mount. Touch fabric adhesive to the edges of the mount and with the design uppermost on a flat surface, place the mount, centrally or as directed, onto the design. At this stage you can pad the design with a little wadding to bring it forward in the mount and soften the edges of the cut-out area. To do this, cut a piece of lightweight wadding just a little larger than the aperture of the mount, touch with glue and fix to the reverse of the embroidered piece. Next glue around the edges of the back of the card or mount backing board and attach it to the back of the embroidery, enclosing the design. Take your time, I have seen too many examples of beautiful stitchwork ruined by bad mounting.

Pots and jars

Back your work with iron-on interfacing before placing in the mount. This has a dual purpose a) it will help prevent fraying and b) it will enable the design to sit more firmly in the mount and not crumple. Iron the interfacing on before you trim the fabric to size. Follow the manufacturers' instructions to assemble the mounts, which are usually simply a matter of trimming the embroidery to fit and placing it in the jar or pot with the backing material in a particular sequence.

Pictures

It is well worth paying for professional mounting. All the effort you have put into the stitching deserves the best!

I like to stretch my work over lightweight wadding as I think it gives a good relief, softening the lines and pushing the stitching forward. A professional framer will lace the work with the wadding over the backing board for you.

A FINAL WORD

Do keep your work in a bag in between stitching: the fabric does tend to pick up dust. But most importantly, after all the rules of 'do's and don'ts', enjoy your craft, be experimental and have fun with creating and stitching the heirlooms of the future!

ACKNOWLEDGEMENTS
My grateful thanks to the following people for their invaluable help and assistance in the writing of this book:

Jean Elliot for the loan of part of her private collection of samplers from which I have used motifs throughout the volume. Jean's establishment 'Copshaw Kitchen Restaurant' in Newcastleton, Roxburghshire is a pleasure to visit for enthusiasts of needlework, antiques and lovers of good food. Whilst one dines one can peruse the beautiful needlework and decide which antique memento to purchase from her extensive stock.

Mike, Mary and Sarah Gray, the family responsible for Framecraft Miniatures Ltd, Aston, Birmingham for their continuing support in the provision of their wide range of beautiful needlework mounts and accessories and advice.

Impress manufacturing for their provision of cards and card mounts. Cara Wigham and Jane Chamberlain of DMC Creative

World plc for their assistance and DMC's provision of fabric and threads.

To Carol Humphrey of the Textile Dept at the Fitzwilliam Museum, Cambridge and Christine Stevens, Research Assistant at St Fagan's Welsh Folk Museum, Wales, who kindly gave me their time and allowed me to tap their vast knowledge of sampler work.

To the 'ladies who stitch': Lynn Blackledge, Sally Harvey, Sally Mason, Barbara Matthews, Gwen Reah, and Gillian South for their patience and diligent stitching of the projects to a standard which puts my own efforts to shame.

To Rosemary Wilkinson, without whom this series would never have come to fruition and for her patience with a disorganized designer. Also Mike Spiller of 'Pentrix Design' for his patience in trying to decipher my scribbles.

And lastly, to my partner, Mike McCabe and children, Sarah, Jonathan and Gareth

for their support for my addiction to the craft and understanding of my neglect for them during the writing of this series.

The Publishers would like to thank the following people for their help in supplying props for photography:
Past Times, Witney, Oxon, OX8 6BH, UK

Market Square (Warminster) Ltd, Wing Farm, Longbridge Deverill, Warminster, Wiltshire BA12 7DD

STOCKISTS
Brooch; Sal-Em products; pots; tray; dressing table set; lacy bookmark; desk pen set; collector's cabinet: Framecraft Miniatures Ltd

Workbox: Market Square

Greetings cards; gift tags: Impress

KITS
All the stitched projects within this book may be purchased in kit form (excluding charts) from: Stitchkits, 8 Danescourt Road, Tettenhall, Wolverhampton, WV6 9BG, UK

PHOTOGRAPH CREDITS
p. 11 Eastnor Castle/Bridgeman Art Library; p. 81 V & A Museum/Bridgeman Art Library; p. 13, p. 75 Museum für Volkskunde, Berlin; p. 14 from 'The Silber and Fleming Glass and China Book', Wordsworth Publications; p. 16 from 'Wallpapers 17th Century to the Present Day', by Joanna Banham, Studio Editions, 1990; p. 17, p. 36, p. 51, p. 85 Jean Elliot, photograph by Ken Taylor; p. 27 (top) Courtesy of the Trustees of the British Museum; p. 27 (lower), p. 42, p. 47, p. 70 Courtesy of the Trustees, Victoria and Albert Museum; p. 29 from 'Le Livre des Abécédaires', © Modes et Travaux; p. 53, p. 76 National Museum of Wales; p. 57, p. 58 Fitzwilliam Museum, Cambridge; p. 62, 87 from 'William Morris Wallpapers', Studio Editions, 1989; p. 66 Christie's Images, London; p. 68 Photographie Giraudon; p. 73 from 'A History of Postcards' by Martin Willoughby, Studio Editions; p. 74 Martin Harrison; p. 82 Fine Art Photographs.
Cover: Angelo Hornak Library